QUILT AS *INSPIRED*™
SMALL SECTIONS. PLAYFUL QUILTING. SMOOTH ASSEMBLY.

VOLUME I
NORDIC LOG CABIN
AND
FLOWERS ON COURTHOUSE STEPS

ANN MYHRE

All rights reserved. No part of this book may be reproduced, stored in any retrieval system, or transmitted in any form or by any means with out the written consent of the author.

Text, artwork and photography © 2016,
Author, Ann Myhre

Quilt As *Inspired*, Volume I/by Ann Myhre
ISBN 978-0692689929
Quilt As Inspired

ACKNOWLEDGEMENT
To All Quilters.
Who have and who continue to share their inspiration and expertise with those of us who love the art and craft of quilt making. I thank you. By sharing techniques and helping others grow their skills, we can all learn from each other and make our community even greater.

And to my own close circle of crafty friends, I am grateful to have you in my life.
Nobody get us but us.

In Memory Of
Grandpa Bud.
Whose blue eyes always twinkled with
tears of joy and pride over everything I ever did.
I miss you every day.

DEDICATION
My Husband and Best Friend, Blain.
Who believes in me and supports without question all of my crazy endeavors.
And who keeps me happy, healthy and hydrated.
I would be lost without you.

My Sons, Josh and Grant.
I can hardly believe my good fortune that I
get to be your mom. You both are incredibly supportive, encouraging and understanding of
my unconventional ways and put up with a less than perfectly-kept house.
I am exceedingly proud of the men you have become.
My heart is full and mind at ease.
May we always play together in Neverland.

My Mom, Cathy
Who jumps with me on every bandwagon I chase.
No matter how fast it's going.
Ain't we got fun.
I am forever grateful for the time and support you always seem to have for me.

Grandma Midge
My entire stream of childhood memories includes you and Grandpa.
If every individual could have people in their life that love and believe in them like you have always done for me, the world would be a better place.
I cherish every moment we still get to spend together.

My Dad, Bob
Every little girl should have a man like you that she can call Daddy.
You have always been and still are that man for me.

I am incredibly fortunate and eternally grateful to live this life with each of you.

Table of Contents

INTRODUCTION:	Just a Bit About Me	1
ABOUT THIS BOOK:	A Non-Conventional Approach to Quilt Making	2
GETTING STARTED:	Pep Talk and Practice	4
INSPIRATION:	Theme, Color, Style, Design, Materials	9
THE QUILTING:	Stitches To Complement the Design	10
PROJECT 1:	**NORDIC LOG CABIN:**	14
	Section One: Drawn, Stitched, Colored	16
	Section Two: Hand Basted, Hand Stitched Applique	20
	Section Three: Wool Applique and Embroidery	26
	Section Four: Fair Isle Strips	32
	Section Five: Patchwork and Painting	34
	Section Six: Dala-Floda Embroidery	41
	Section Seven: Glue-Basted Hand Pieced Hexies	48
	Section Eight: Nordic Star Altered Blocks	54
	Section Nine: Border Strips and White Work	57
	Section Ten: Log Cabin Inside the Log Cabin	60
	Section Eleven: Little Cabin in the Woods	63
	Section Twelve: Fusible Floral Motifs, Machine Applique	72
	Section Thirteen: Couching the Trip around the World	78
	Finishing: Frame Border	80
	Reflection: Looking at the Whole Picture	81
PROJECT 2:	**FLOWERS ON COURTHOUSE STEPS**	82
	Section One: Patchwork Tulips: Y-seams.	83
	Section Two: Blended Angles	90
	Section Three: Blended Angles/Freezer Paper Applique	94
	Section Four: Sugar Bowl Blocks with Broderie Perse	102
	Section Five: Flower Baskets, X-Blocks and Applique	106
	Section Six: Free Motion Fabric Borders	114
	Section Seven: Free Motion Fabric Borders/Hand Applique	115
	Finishing: Traditional Binding, Labels, Sleeves	118
CONCLUSION:	Until Next Time…	120

INTRODUCTION

"I send my quilt tops out to the longarmer."
"Why?" I asked.
They'd answer, "Because I can't quilt it myself."

Although I was curious, I didn't have much experience with quilting, so I shrugged it off and just kept knitting and crocheting. I owned a busy knit shop at the time, and quilting was not my focus. But a few years later, when I introduced fabric to the store so knitters could make bag linings and accessories to coordinate with their knits, I had a flood of quilters coming in to shop the cotton prints I brought in. Unbeknownst to me, these fabrics were perfect for contemporary quilt making.

At that point, my experience with quilting was limited to a pieced Christmas block sampler I did in my mid-twenties that was tucked in a drawer somewhere and, almost a decade later (2002), a paper-pieced garden quilt for my Grandma Midge's 75th birthday. Grandma loves hummingbirds and flowers so I, completely clueless, went over to a big box store, grabbed a book about paper piecing a perfect garden (having no idea what paper piecing was), got some cute calico fabrics and just worked through it step by step. I arranged the blocks into a 3'x5' quilt top. I then sandwiched it with poly batting, ditched it and free motion stippled it on my brand new Janome that my husband bought for me after I swore quilting was going to be my new big venture. I didn't know a single quilter and had no idea there was such a thing as a longarm machine or that I could send it out for someone else to quilt it. Ignorance is bliss. I had so much fun making it and even more fun giving it. My grandma was thrilled and it hangs proudly in her living room to this day. It isn't perfect and that's okay. She loves it. I wasn't going for perfect. I was going for a token of love and admiration for one of my favorite people on earth. Mission accomplished. I couldn't wait to make more.

Then, boom! I opened a knit shop. In the early 2000s, I was learning to knit, along with everyone else at the time, and by April, 2003, Knitty Cat in Centennial, Colorado, was open. It was an overnight success. With great timing on hitting a trend and an around-the-clock work schedule, I found myself caught up in a flurry of new knitters and in making overnight yarn orders to keep the shelves full. I had a wonderful community of loyal customers and made lifelong friends. Finally, after 11 years of an exhausting business, I closed the shop and was left with a great supply of specialty yarns and cotton fabrics, and finally, the time I had been craving to pursue personal artwork and design. I am now quilting (obsessively), and have met hundreds of quilters. I still find that a great majority of quilters feel intimidated to quilt their own quilts.

ABOUT THIS BOOK

I get it now. It's scary. It can be daunting to have a finished top that you invested much time, love and energy into just to see the words "quilt as desired" at the end of a pattern. Not to mention the physical demands of squaring up an enormous top and pushing it through a domestic sewing machine. After struggling through the quilting of a couple of large quilts this way, I am now fully aware of what a longarm machine is and understand exactly why people send their quilts out. Holy smokes those things are super cool! I tried one at a quilt show once and it just sailed smoothly across the surface making perfect stitches effortlessly. But I don't have room for a longarm machine, the cost of one is steep, and I want to quilt my projects on the domestic machine I've already invested in. So I was determined to learn the intricate stitches that people with those wonderful longarm machines can do.

Being fairly new to quilting, not knowing many of the "rules" and not being the kind of girl who would likely follow them anyway, I developed a way to create my bigger quilts section by section. An enhanced quilt-as-you-go process, if you will. I have researched different ways that quilters long before us have stitched their quilts in smaller sections and then put them together; however, I haven't found many actual patterns. Perhaps it's because there are a few limitations for quilting in this way. Despite that, I've decided to overcome those hurdles and make it my mission to create fun quilt patterns that we can manage more easily. Essentially, we take a main idea, gather materials that meet the theme, and build the quilt one section at a time utilizing as many different techniques as we'd like. Rather than leave the quilting to the end as a daunting task or have someone else execute the stitching for us, we include the actual quilting as we create, being inspired by not only the quilt as a whole, but also by the section we're currently making. And just like that, my concept, Quilt As Inspired™, was born. And I'm so excited to share this alternative style of quilt making with you.

This book is for the beginning quilter to the person who may have pieced many a top but hasn't had much success in the quilting process or much experience in playing with different techniques. I have tried to keep the writing conversational, as if I were with you in a workshop or one-on-one lesson. It is more like a journal of my thoughts, design process and consequently, the steps taken to create the projects. I want this creative endeavor you're about to embark on to be joyful and pleasant. Keep in mind, we are not performing life-saving surgery here. Writing it out, it sounds obvious, but it's very easy to get caught up in the process and take ourselves too seriously about what is supposed to be enjoyable. I promise that by working in smaller, more manageable sections, you can learn to quilt beautiful linear and free motion patterns with a lot less effort and a lot more fun. And I will cheer you on every stitch of the way. If you ever get confused or get lost in project, please feel free to contact me by email - visit my site (www.annmyhrequilts.com) to get my current information. I will answer you as soon as possible as I am (almost) always connected. My number one goal is for you to find success and joy in quilt making. Also, visit my YouTube channel, Quilt As Inspired, where you'll find a few videos to help give clarity on certain techniques that may be difficult to learn without watching someone else demonstrate them.

After working through the practice exercise, you'll find two different types of quilt projects that each shows my detailed step-by-step journey to create them. In the first quilt, Nordic Log Cabin, you'll learn both traditional piecing, as well as more freeform techniques such as painting, embroidery and couching. The Nordic Log Cabin is perfect for the bohemian arts and crafts lover who might have a large collection (stash) of different fabrics, yarns and threads. If you enjoy cross-crafting, mixing patterns and creating heavy texture with hand stitching as much as I do, this one's for you. The second quilt, Flowers on Courthouse Steps, is a more conventional project made with patchwork and applique, ideal for someone who likes a more traditional looking, symmetrical quilt. You'll find more precise directions here than with my freestyle approach to the Nordic quilt.

For both projects, you'll get suggested quilting patterns and a couple of different ways to attach each quilted piece. This method allows for many different design opportunities to employ in your quilts. If you have an idea that you like better than a given pattern for a certain section, please try it. These improv quilts are like a choose-your-own adventure with no master plan. Instead, there is a vision or inspiration and a set of design guidelines for each quilt. No more piecing backs, squaring up large pieces, or back-breaking quilting for me. I've developed this method not only to avoid the unpleasantness that comes with quilting a monster, but also because I love to work on many different techniques all at once. My intention is to help you give yourself permission to play and tell your own story through improv quilt making. While there are only two main projects, each one has a ton of techniques and quilting patterns to use and adapt in countless future projects. My hope is that you will find inspiration and come up with your own ideas so that you can always "Quilt As *Inspired*."

Last, but certainly not least, free motion quilting is not second nature when starting out. For anyone. Even with my can-do attitude and fearless free spirit, I initially questioned whether I could actually be good at free motion stitching. I struggled pretty badly at first, and at one time, even priced out longarm machines! But then I remembered how awkward knitting was in the beginning. Now I can knit in the dark in the park in the rain on a train. The key to success when trying any new skill is to not expect perfection from yourself, have faith that you will succeed, and trust that you will gain the blindly-acquired and priceless benefits of the muscle memory you will build during the hours you practice. There is a theory that 10,000 hours of focused practice of any skill will help you to achieve mastery. While I'm not sure there is an exact formula that covers every activity, I guarantee that if you spend even 100 hours, on true, focused quilting (not piecing), you will become really good at it, and perhaps, even master it. Don't believe me? Have a little faith, put your resolve face on, and let's jump in with both feet.

GETTING STARTED

When approaching any large project and feel overwhelmed, the best way to tackle it is to break it down. We're going to do just that with quilt making. Below are some basic things to keep in mind while we play with this alternative style of making a quilt.

The Quilt Police.

There are so many different ways to make quilts. Ever hear of the quilt police? Please keep in mind they have no authority, are unable to obtain a search warrant, and therefore cannot legally search your quilts for any wrongdoing. It is your right (constitutional even) to make anything you want the way you see fit. The only law you must follow is to enjoy quilt making. Sound silly? So does the concept of quilt police.

Play
Experiment
Enjoy your own creativity
Do your best work
Perfection is overrated.
Let it be
Have fun
Be yourself. No one else can do it nearly as well. You do you!

Machine Basics.

You don't need a fancy machine to quilt. Any machine that you can attach a darning (free motion) foot and lower the feed dogs will do. If you can't lower your dogs, I've heard of people taping cardboard over them and setting stitch length to 0. If you're in the market for a machine, the **must have** features to get are: needle down, an extension table (clear ones will also function as a light box), & the ability to drop your feed dogs. Get free motion, ¼ inch, and walking feet.

So Much to Learn. So Much to Buy.

All of the information you're about to read on threads, needles, batting, tension settings, fabrics etc. does not have to be retained or remembered. Every quilting scenario will need to be worked out and practiced before you even touch your project.

You'll be collecting lots of different notions as you learn different techniques. If you're new to this, get the basics: a 24x36" rotary mat, rotary cutter, good scissors, 24x6" clear ruler, Frixion pen, Sewline chalk pencil, seam ripper, iron, pressing surface, pressing cloth, various needles, good pins.

My Biggest Piece of Advice

Super important. ALWAYS have a small (8"x8" or so) practice sandwich handy by your machine. A quilt sandwich for this purpose would be made of a solid fabric on top (or a print that you can practice outlining), a piece of batting you are using in the project you're practicing for and a random cotton backing. Any time you sit down to begin working on your project, first just doodle some leaves, flowers, your name, whatever on this sandwich. It's a good way to get your free motion groove on and test your tension (and the machine's tension. Wink).

The Skinny on Threads and Needles

Holy Choices Batman! The varieties of needles and threads on the market are overwhelming to say the very least. When buying thread, look at the spool information. The most important number is the weight (30, 40, 50, 60, 100 most common)

The smaller the number = the heavier the thread.

Knowing what you are using on your project is crucial to the success of it. The ply is important as well. A 2ply thread is generally thinner than a 3ply. When in doubt of what you're buying, ask your local quilt shop. They know their stuff. The threads listed below all come from quilt shops – the big box threads are ok, but if you want superior quality (and you do) spend a bit more and support your LQS.

PRO TIP: When quilting, or thread painting, always use the same weight or thinner thread in the bobbin or you'll get bobbin thread peekies on the top (unless you're doing bobbin work which is a whole other thing).

You have to experiment to find what you love. That's what I did and below are my favorites and why. My way is certainly not the only way, but it works for me and might be a good jumping off point for you.

Piecing: Aurafil cotton 50/2. Lots of colors, strong but thin enough for non-bulky seams. No fuzzies. Grippy enough to hold stitches together. Awesome for applique and micro stipple quilting too.

Thread painting/Quilting:
Mettler Silk Finish cotton 50/3. Lots of colors, thick enough to see the stitches, and fills the hole of a size 75 or 80 quilting needle beautifully. Matte finish.
Robison-Anton 40/2. Lots of colors, a bit thinner than Mettler because of the ply, despite the weight. Beautiful sheen if shimmer is your thing. This comes on a cone-shaped spool. Whenever using thread that comes in a cone shape, I'll use a vertical spool holder that sits on the side of my machine. These are cheap at the big box stores and are critical when using cone thread. Get one for sure even if you have a vertical spool holder on your machine. Sometimes that sits too high and the thread doesn't come off the top properly.
Superior King Tut 40/3. Favorite multi-color quilting thread to be sure.
Superior Tire Silk 30. So expensive. So worth it. Gorgeous impact – get a few colors from Superior online.
Sulky Rayon 30. A beautiful shimmering thick thread that is as beautiful as the silk for a fraction of the price.
Monofilament 60. When I just want stitch impressions without thread color, I'll use clear on top and bottom. Loosen up those tension disks and practice with this thread!

In the Bobbin: My ideal quilting set up is Mettler cotton on top and a like-color Aurafil thread in the bobbin as it's thinner and lasts longer. Any more, I love to see the different threads I used on the back – it makes kind of a secondary design that is really pretty and worth the bobbin changing effort. If you're using a busy back and don't want to change bobbin colors all the time, use a thin monofilament thread from Aurafil, YLI or madeira – 50 or 60 weight is ideal (just thinner than top thread). Smoke color for dark backs/clear for light.

PRO TIP: I NEVER try to match the bobbin thread to the color of the backing fabric without regard to the top thread when free motion quilting. It may not play nicely with all the top threads that I might be using. Any tension issues will show on both sides and cause hours of hair pulling frustration. Ask me how I know.

Needles: Another thing to overwhelm you. I'll keep it short. The eye of your needle needs to be completely filled but not stuffed with the thread. My general practice:

75/11 quilting or Microtex sharps 80/12 for piecing, thread embroidery and quilting with thread weights 40 and 50.

90/14 or 100/16 topstitch or denim for 30 weight threads and lots of thread embellishment.

60/8 sharp needle for thin micro quilting or delicate stitching with 60 to 100 weight threads.

A Bit of Free Motion Practice:

Let's do this. No pressure. Just playing around. No big deal. On a 6"x10" sandwich, I stitched an orange leaf, yellow daisy, cream heart, multi feather, and a teal bloopy. Just like a bowl of Lucky Charms! I used 5 different top and bobbin threads in order to address this whole crazy tension thing. I used a Schmetz Microtex 80/12 needle, grey cotton fabric, cotton batting, and muslin back. The top row of motifs shown below was done with top threads that were paired with a like-color thread in the bobbin. The entire bottom row of motifs was done with the same threads listed as the top row but with Aurafil monofilament thread in the bobbin.

Threads Used – top row of sample:

Orange leaf: Mettler 50wt silk finish cotton top/Robison-Anton 40wt rayon in bobbin.
Yellow daisy: Janome 40wt rayon embroidery top/Mettler 50wt silk finish cotton bobbin.
Cream heart: Sulky 40wt rayon embroidery top/prewound poly bobbin spool.
Multi feather: Aurafil 50wt 2ply multi thread top/same for the bobbin.
Teal bloopy: Sulky 30wt rayon embroidery top/Mettler 50wt silk finish cotton bobbin.

Tension settings (my default tension is 4.6):

Orange leaf: top tension at 3.8 when using the rayon bobbin/3.6 with the monofilament.
Yellow daisy: top tension was 3.4 for both bobbin threads.
Cream heart: top tension to 4.2 for the prewound bobbin and 3.6 for the monofilament.
Multi feather: top tension was 3.2 for the matching thread, and 3.6 for the monofilament.
Teal leaf: top was 3.0 for the colorful bobbin thread and 3.6 for the monofilament.

Do not feel like you have to run out and get the exact threads I used. The purpose of this practice is to show that different threads on top and bottom will require different tension settings. And your machine will probably use different tension settings than mine. I am currently sewing on a Viking Topaz 30. All machines are different and so it's important that you spend some time getting to know yours. Most people will say not to mess with your bottom tension. Unless you are very comfortable with your machine, I tend to agree that it isn't necessary and recommend that you stick with adjusting the top tension only. Keep a tension journal by your machine and take notes. By the way, I do not have nor have I ever used a stitch regulator. I'm sure they're great, but I love the idea of doing all the work myself, and with a bit of practice, you'll find that you don't really need one.

First and foremost, relax. Perhaps play some flowing, mellow music. Grab a glass of wine or favorite beverage and put on your game face. Whether this is your very first time free motion stitching or it's been a while, it will take a minute to get into the zone. Remember to breathe. **Don't rush this.**

Slow your machine down if you can. I have mine set at 2/5 speed
Put on your free motion (darning) foot
Lower your feed dogs (or if not possible, cover them with tape and cardboard)
Set stitch length to 0 or lowest setting (normal setting is usually around 2.5)
If your machine has this ability, set machine in 'needle up' to pull up bobbin thread (see below)
Set 'needle down' after bobbin thread is pulled to top

Draw shapes if you wish. I usually don't mark for practice, as I want the freedom to play. If you decide to draw, use a Frixion pen (erases with the heat of your iron) or the Sewline mechanical chalk pencil. Place the sandwich under your needle and always draw up the bobbin thread:

Hold top thread with left hand   Needle down/up, pull thread up   Stitch a bit. Clip both together.

Always do this when starting any new thread for quilting. These threads will drive you nutty if you don't clip them. Make a few tiny stitches at first to lock them in, stitch your pattern for a few inches, gently tug the tails, then clip them together. When ending a thread, turn quilt WS up, tug the bobbin thread so top thread comes up through the back. Weave them in as you go to avoid a hot mess.

> **Leaf**: I started at the base just below the stem. I stitched down to the point of the leaf (cut my threads), then back up to start. I then went up and did the stem, met back down at start, did the little inside detail, back up to start, then did the wavy outer lines. Just follow the lines if you drew them, or meander.
>
> **Feathers**: There are lots of ways to do feathers. Every quilter does them differently. I start at the stem of the feather and stitch up the spine and make a top loop, then I continue making loops back down to the base, I then stitch up the other side of the spine to that first top loop and come back down the other side with loops to the base. Some quilters just make one line for the spine, some do 3, some do no spine at all. You'll find your own way and isn't what this is all about? But it takes a ton of practice.
>
> Please see my YouTube channel for a demonstration of these practice shapes.

This may seem really scary – even on your practice piece. But perspective alert! We are not disarming bombs here so wipe that sweat off your brow. Practice. Breathe. Relax. Play.

Now cut your threads and really look at the piece. It is completely normal if your stitches go from incredibly tiny to totally huge. You're a new at this. It's more than likely a speed of the machine vs. speed of your hands thing. Now look at the back. If you see a very tight string with "whiskers," particularly around curves you need to slow your hands down and maybe look at tension. Look below to my collection of personal pitfalls and my solutions. I'd be shocked if you didn't have whiskers. I still get them at times, hence the starter sandwich that lives by my machine. If all looks well, keep going. Fill that 6"x10" piece with all kinds of shapes and doodles. You are just practicing to gain confidence here. Remember, all this practice stitching is getting you comfy cozy for your future as a free-motion quilter!

TROUBLESHOOTING

Bird's Nest on Back. You either have threads you didn't bring up to the top or weaved in and they got caught in bobbin case OR your top thread needs to be rethreaded. Make sure your presser foot is all the way up before threading. Those tension discs need to be open to properly thread. The other cause of this is you forgot to lower your presser foot. I do it all the time.

Dots of bobbin thread on top. Your thread tension is too tight and is pulling your bobbin thread up to the front of the work. Lower your top tension 2 clicks at a time. Remember to keep the bobbin thread the same or thinner.

Dots of top thread or whiskers on back. Your top thread tension needs to be snugged up a bit. It is sometimes difficult to correct this especially if you're new, as this could be caused by speeding around the curves. If using a solid back, match your thread color and you won't even see the dots. If you see thread whiskers, we need to take care of this. However, there is no magic formula. It takes practice to hit the sweet spot. See loss of control below. Remember learning to drive a stick shift? How you thought you would never get it? But then you kept trying and now it's second nature? Yep. And don't even get me started on learning how to golf. Maddening.

Miniscule stitches. Your machine is going way too fast and your hands aren't keeping up. Easiest fix – slow your machine down. This is not a race. Channel your inner tortoise.

Monster long stitches. You're in a hurry to get this over with! Slow your hands down to a more comfortable pace and enjoy the stitching. This was my biggest hurdle. I got so excited when I knew where I wanted to go, I speed raced over to it and cheated my fabric out of beautiful stitching in the process. I try to remember that I'm not drawing with a pen, I am stitching with a needle that is moving up and down at the same speed at all times. Let it do what it's supposed to. Stitch. The fabric needs to be moved along at the same pace the whole time.

Feeling a loss of control. Your hands are trying to match the speed of the machine. It is totally natural to want to do this. **You'll find your comfort zone somewhere in the place where the machine is going a bit faster than your hands are moving.** Again, don't try to match your movement with the machine, just keep the machine at the same speed as itself and relax and slow your hands down a bit. This is HUGE. I was teaching my mom and noticed her in what looked like an uncontrolled frenzy trying speed her hands up with the machine. I said, "Mom! Slow your hands down!" So she kept the machine at the same pace and slowed her fabric movement down a bit. It was like turning on a light switch. I cannot tell you enough how this helped her in a manner of seconds. This was a huge teaching moment for me and a revelation for her. She's so happy with her stitching now and so am I. Keep trying. You'll get it. I pinky promise.

Any quilting master (or master of anything, really) will tell you. They focused intensely and practiced tenaciously. Ability isn't a gift. It's earned.

INSPIRATION
Theme, Color, Style, Design, Materials

While I have given specific instructions for both quilts in the chapters to follow, you may want to use them as a guide to make a quilt with your own ideas or inspiration. Below are some factors to keep in mind when creating quilts with your own unique vision.

Every quilt begins with an inspiration. It could be color, shape, theme, style, etc. It is important to know why you are making or designing a particular quilt so you can truly learn what makes **you** swoon. There are so many choices in fabrics, colors and styles of quilts that even the most accomplished quilt maker can easily feel overwhelmed. Narrowing down what sends that true jolt of inspiration through you will help you stay on track with the design decisions for your piece.

You may want to make a quilt based on a family vacation you took to the beach, or of your beloved pet or a day trip to the botanic gardens. This quilting method can easily be made to interpret your own vision. All you need are memories, pictures or memorabilia from a certain time or place, a color pallet and a big quilters toolbox filled with the skills you'll acquire as you take classes and workshops, and with my most sincere hope, working through this book. Keep an open mind and an open journal. Anyone can do this as the sections can be made to fit any skill level.

Sometimes it's really easy. You're making a gift for a child who loves dinosaurs. Or you see a quilt at the quilt shop, fall in love, buy the kit and make it. Or you join a block of the month club with a friend. All valid reasons to make a quilt. Any reason is a valid reason to make a quilt. What is important is to know what *your* reason is. Focus on why you've chosen to make the quilts you've made in the past. That way, when it comes time to designing your own project, you have a good handle on what it will take to realize your vision. The main thing to keep in mind is that you are making a quilt that makes you happy. The world wants to see you shine. We can't help but look and admire you for being you. Don't try to please everyone (we all know that doesn't work). As I design the quilts in this book, I am well aware that my boho aesthetic will not be for everyone. And I'm completely at peace with that. As long as my heart is happy while working, all is well. It's about the journey. The end result will be what it wants to be. Your freedom of expression will make your quilts special. Isn't that what all this is all about, anyway?

You'll want to consider the style and layout for your inspiration. That will depend a lot on where the quilt will live when it's done. Is it a wall quilt or one for the bed? Is it an artful t-shirt quilt going with a college child? Your formal living room for decor? The mountain house? The answers to these kinds of questions will winnow down your choices for constructing the quilt and make it easier to stay within certain confines so you'll get a successful project in the end. All these questions will get you thinking about your own creativity. Ideas will form and the design process will happen as you work the projects in the coming pages. Best to keep that inspiration journal handy.

QUILTING
STITCHES TO COMPLEMENT THE DESIGN

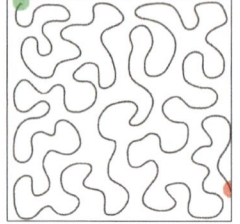    

When designing, a few considerations need to be made on the quilting. Thread choice, density, all-over, dot-to-dot, echo, motif, etc. The possibilities are endless. I can tell you with confidence that these decisions are so much easier to make and execute when you have smaller pieces to work on. Above are doodles I did in Sketchbook Pro on my iPad. Sometimes when I just don't feel like doing anything major, I'll doodle quilt designs and save them. Later, I can scroll through them, email one to myself and make it any size I want. It's good clean fun.

WHERE DO I START?

My initial approach is to stick with the theme of the quilt. For example, if I'm making a modern quilt, I wouldn't stitch a bunch of precious roses all over it or stipple too densely in lots of colors as straight lines and negative space are important to achieve modernism.

You can always rely on its intended use. If it is an art quilt that will hang on the wall, lots of dense quilting and embellishment can be applied as it never will be used or washed. Alternatively, a bed or sofa quilt shouldn't have too much dense stitching as it will lose snuggle factor. We want our quilts to be admired, fought over and well used by our loved ones. Not to mention, machine washed without trauma.

Here, we'll be thinking about the actual quilt pattern as we work because we are quilting each section as we create, making sure it is going to enhance the finished project. How?

We Quilt As *Inspired*!

IS THERE A RIGHT OR WRONG?

The fabrics you choose and patterns made by piecing can also dictate the quilting design. You may want to duplicate a motif in one of the fabrics, or quilt little stipples, or cross hatch within the confines of the blocks. For each project, I will take you through my thought process on the quilting to help you start embarking on your own journey of the quilting path.

Don't restrict yourself by using only what I've provided on the quilting. What I have chosen is dictated by what I have learned in my short time as a quilter or by simply what makes sense to me. What I've put forward may not jive with your aesthetic. It is completely okay if you want to try something different or if you'd like to simplify or beef up any of the designs.

There is no right or wrong.

It's YOUR quilt!

Here are some further topics that will need your attention when you're ready to design quilts. Below are the basics that will be discussed in further detail with each section.

TO MARK OR NOT TO MARK. THAT IS THE QUESTION.

My general rule is that if the quilt pattern is linear, geometric, or symmetrical, and it may be obvious if my lines wander, I'll mark it. With an organic pattern where I'm stitching leaves, flowers or wavy lines, I don't bother.

Laziness kicks in for me when it comes time for marking so I only do it if I have to. Plus I come at quilting from a folk art perspective so those little human touches and original design worked by eye without the aid of rulers and purchased gadgets, that I can never find or remember that I have, makes me happy and gets me far from trying to achieve perfection.

In any event, I always practice the line by drawing it first on paper. I cannot stress enough how important this is for getting the design into your head and hand.

THE PENS. DIFFERENT STROKES FOR DIFFERENT FOLKS (or fabrics).

I love a Frixion pen on light color fabrics. Anything that will erase instantaneously with the heat of an iron is the pen for me. However. If you use a Frixion on darker fabrics and erase the line, you will see a faint white residue from the gel itself. In other words, the ink disappears, but the residue does not. I am not bothered by this as my quilts are so busy. Also, the ink can reappear in very cold temperatures. I put a sample in the freezer and faint ink lines did reappear. But they went away again with a swipe of the iron.

For dark color fabrics I use the Sewline mechanical chalk pencil in white that can be brushed or washed away. This gives a nice fine line for intricate marking. I've heard that the other colors don't wash away as well as the white. But white is all we need so it's all good.

BATTING. TOO MANY CHOICES TO DRIVE YOU BATTY.

As you experiment with different batting choices, you'll be able to choose the best material for the project you're making. My favorite batting for a usable bed quilt is wool. It might be a bit more expensive but the loft is awesome and shows all the patterning you've worked so hard to achieve. When doing larger pieces, you'll notice that wool is much more manageable because of its loft and is lightness. Poly is great for these reasons too, but you're trading warmth for durability. You can machine wash wool batting in delicate but can wash a poly quilt like crazy.

I'll use silk, bamboo or a very thin loft cotton if I want a lighter bed cover or a wall hanging. The great thing about quilting in sections, is it's a good way to use up small leftovers of whatever you have. I've been known to use 3 or 4 different battings within one quilt. It adds to the different textures we can achieve. Ultimately, (as with any decision making for the project) the answer of which batting to choose lies with the intended use of the quilt.

THREAD
COLOR AND WEIGHT

You probably already have a type of quilting that you are drawn to. I love it when the thread matches or is a shade lighter or darker than the fabric. That way the stitches still stand out but don't overpower the design. Not to mention that a contrasting thread will show EVERYTHING.

Monofilament (clear) thread is a great choice if you just want the texture to show without additional color. It's tricky to use. Make time to practice. I find that I have to slow my movement down at times or even mess with my bobbin tension (gulp).

Multi-colored thread has to be chosen wisely – things can look really weird if part of the thread shows and the other part of the colors blend within the quilt. I happen to love multicolored thread and have learned the hard way – many times over – that for me, it's better in thread painting. Practice practice practice. There are lots of choices in thread that will work in your project – but don't leave it up to chance.

And no one says you have to pick just one – Within any given section, you can choose several solid threads to "color" your design. This was my approach to the Nordic Log Cabin. It's bohemian and whimsical.
Like me.

DENSITY.
WHO'S USING THIS QUILT ANYWAY?

When a quilt is quilted all at once, a careful eye has to be on keeping the amount of quilting pretty much the same over the surface of the quilt so that it will lay flat. For example, say you want to do some heavy quilting in the middle of the quilt to embellish flowers with vines and leaves and petals, etc., you'll have to continue the same amount of quilting over the whole quilt or it could be wavy and crazy.

With the Quilt As *Inspired* approach, you can quilt anything on any section because you'll be trimming and squaring up **before** it gets added to the main piece. The amount of quilting then becomes less a matter of function and more a matter of aesthetics.

My general rule is to work macro then micro. In other words, baste the edges, ditch the seams or larger sections to stabilize, then go back and work smaller more detailed quilting on each stabilized section. That way you'll get less slipping and sliding around. The more control the better when free motion quilting. Not only that, as you stabilize, you'll get better acquainted and less intimidated by the section and may be pleasantly surprised at the quilting ideas that pop into your head just by handling the fabric.

    I am always amazed by this.

> *****WHATEVER YOU DECIDE…*****
> **DON'T**
>
> …add any additional free motion quilting on the main piece regardless of how many sections are attached. All the quilting should be done on the current section you're working on. Once you're satisfied with the way it looks, go ahead and add it to the main quilt. You can add embellishments, applique, or hand stitching if you feel like a section just needs a little something extra. I do this all the time – sometimes planned even. But running it under your machine for free motion will inevitably make your piece wonky and won't lay flat. Another ask me how I know moment. You may be tempted. Don't do it.

> **YOUR OWN ABILITY.**
> **COMFORT VS. ADVENTURE.**
>
> This is the golden key to the design decision making. The deal breaker, so to speak.
>
> In the Inspiration and Quilting sections of the book, I've given a lot of information that may or may not make sense to you at this point. My intention is to touch on the important factors that you'll want to consider when designing and store it on the backburner until you're ready to create your own quilting adventure. My hope is that you'll come back to these sections when you're at that point. If you find yourself a bit over-informed, don't worry. You don't need to understand all of this before working the projects to come. In depth knowledge can only come with experience. Just knowing that many options are available to a person in the quilting stage is essential. But can also be completely overwhelming and intimidating, so all any of us will likely do is work within our comfort zone. That zone can only expand by doing and playing. This method will allow you to play with different threads, colors and styles of quilting without committing all that experimentation over one large surface. Plus, let's face it, pushing a huge quilt through a domestic machine all at once is very unpleasant. I don't plan on doing that ever again.

> **THE SAVING GRACE.**
>
> The beauty of this method is that even if you piece or quilt something that doesn't turn out the way you visualized it (this will happen and still does to me), it's not catastrophic – you're working each section separately from your main piece so you can't mess up what you've already done. Don't get discouraged. Sometimes we just can't know what something is going to look like until we just dive in and do it. More often than not, the result will be even better than you'd hoped for. But even if you make a piece that doesn't fit in, you can save it for later. No harm done. Your main piece hasn't even been touched. Nothing is a waste of time because everything you do matters in the long run. The experience alone…
> **GO FOR IT!**

NORDIC LOG CABIN
63"x82"

Nothing says Scandinavian folk art like brightly colored embroideries, repetitive handknit patterns and painted floral designs. Inspired by some of the classic motifs from that region, I've used the classic log cabin setting to combine quilt blocks, hand stitching and applique, in an attempt to create the ultimate free-style, contemporary quilt. I picture it on a rustic bed, cheering up a dimly lit cabin in the woods. This is my way of giving a nod to the many exceptionally skilled Nordic artisans who, with their hand crafted pieces, were able to decorate their homes for celebrations with loved ones.

Gradually Gathering Materials.

My inspiration fabric is in the middle and I only have 1/4 yard. It's old and I can't get anymore. But I know going in that I won't need any more than what I have. Instead, I'll be using that fabric to coordinate solids, dots, stripes, tone-on-tones and mini prints to achieve the Nordic folk art look that I'm going for. I'll be adding additional fabrics as I go and probably won't use everything you see here, but having it together in a pile helps me stay within the mood of the piece.

I've also gathered from my stash several colors of wool felt, yarns, embroidery flosses, trims, and threads to execute the designs I have floating around in my head. If you don't have a huge stash of fabrics and threads, don't fret. You'll find a specific materials list at the beginning of each section. Trying to collect everything at once to make this type of improvisational project makes it difficult to keep an open mind, so I tend to just have a starting pallet. As your project grows, you'll find the materials that the quilt begs for. Think of it as an ever evolving entity. To start, have an inspiration fabric, some fat quarters to coordinate, a queen-size amount of batting of your choice (I used wool), about 6 yards of backing fabric and the materials listed for Section 1. The backing doesn't need to be all the same. This can be a great stash buster. Perfect for utilizing what we have, collecting bits and pieces when feeling inspired or don't have to drop hundreds of dollars for one project all at once (true bohemian living).

When you make the time to play (hopefully daily) just be sure to have the materials listed for the current section. It's all about staying in the moment, working with improvisation, tapping into the right side of the brain, and above all else, enjoying your YOU time.

Materials for Section 1:

18" square freezer paper * pencil * Sharpie * lightbox or window * Set of 2 mirrors: Also have some regular copy paper on hand to practice this before going to freezer paper. It will bring comfort.
Fabric marking pen: I used a Frixion Pen to transfer the design.
18" square top fabric: I used white pfd (prepared for dying) cotton. It isn't essential to use pfd, but I had it on hand and it does hold inks and dyes well. You can use and prewash any light color fabric if you're going to color it.
19" square backing fabric * 19" square batting: The extra size allows for wiggle room when trimming.
Tsukineko inks/Fantastix * Fabrico markers * Aloe or other textile medium: These are what I used to color mine. The inks can be a bit costly. Amazon has the best options and prices. Practice with different markers, inks, fabric paints and colored pencils. Always wait 24 hours to dry, heat set (use a pressing cloth) and throw it in the wash.
Quilting thread: I used Robison Anton black rayon thread. It repels inks and won't take on color while painting.

SECTION 1:
THE CENTER PIECE WILL SET THE STAGE.

Step 1: Design it.

Cut an 18" piece of freezer paper from the roll. Fold it in half once paper side out, then fold it in half again so you have a 9" square. Fold it once more this time diagonally so that all the folds come to a point. This is the center of the square. Take your pencil and start drawing lines on the triangle, keeping in mind our inspiration of Nordic arts (or whatever inspiration you're working with). Think scrolls, vines, tulips, hearts etc.

You can do half hearts and flowers on the folds.

*

Make sure most lines are connected or you'll be stitching with lots starts and stops, which is a pain when you're first starting out. I stitched this design in about 5 thread passes.

*

Don't go crazy on the drawing. We do have to stitch this. Feel free to use my example.

*

When you're done, place the point in the corner of two mirrors held together as shown above so you can see the design in its entirety. Draw more lines where needed.

Step 2: Transfer it.

Once you are happy with the entire design, go over the pencil lines with a Sharpie. Go slowly and smooth out any rough lines and get it ready for tracing. Now with your Sharpie, trace the image on to the other 7 sections of the paper by opening and refolding the paper and lining up the drawing to fit the current triangle. You can use a lightbox for this, but with a Sharpie and a white background, you'll probably be able to see well enough without one.

Iron the waxy side of the paper to the wrong side (WS) of your fabric (if there is one). Press both sides to smooth out the wrinkles.

Use your chosen fabric marking pen and put the fabric on a light box, window or glass table with light underneath (I use my machine's extension table and the flashlight from my phone) and trace the entire design. Don't iron until stitched! Your ink will disappear and you'll be furious!

Step 3: Make a Sandwich.

Of course, I am talking about a quilt sandwich with top layer, batting and backing, but hey, if you want to make a real sandwich before you start the stitching, go for it. It's good to have comfort food when about to do something that could be a bit stressful.

Once the design is transferred, remove the freezer paper (save it!) and layer your quilt sandwich. The batting and backing will extend ½" on all sides. Smooth with hands (not iron!), pin corners and then baste with a walking foot and any chosen thread around edges with a 1/8" seam. Remove pins. Attach your free motion/darning foot.

Step 4: Choosing thread.

I used a rayon black thread to outline the design and repel the ink as I color. Black shows every stinkin' little line but gives a wonderful graphic look when the shapes are filled in with color, which also helps hide any weirdo stitch lines. If black or a dark color makes you nervous, you could also use clear or white. Having said that, clear thread is impossible to see where you've stitched.

Consider stitching your design with multiple colors or a multi-color thread. I KNOW you have your practice piece sitting by your machine so of course, you can experiment. Remember, there is no right or wrong.

Step 5: Stitch it.

Start in center and begin to stitch. Remember to pull up that bobbin thread! If you used my design, you'll be able to do the center 4 scroll motifs in one thread. Then cut 6" threads, turn over, tug on the back thread to pull front thread to back, weave both into the batting and clip. Take this time to breathe, stand and stretch. Rejoin at the base of one of the tulip spokes. Each spoke gets its own thread. The outer scrolling can be done in one thread with a bit of traveling (which means going over a previously stitched line) I like to call this piggybacking.

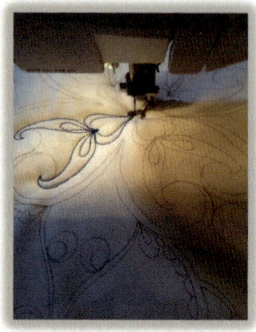 

You are not a robot. Don't get discouraged if you stitch off the lines. It WILL happen. Remember. We are erasing those lines. Look at mine below. You can see lots of misses. Try to view your drawn lines as suggestions.

Add lines to the drawing and stitching as needed. I added an echo line to the bumps shown above right to make the stitching go farther with same thread getting myself back down to the base of the scroll. You don't know 'til you know, ya know?

Step 6: Color it.

You can now iron those drawn lines away. Fabrico markers and Tsukineko inks are of my favorite products as they create bold colors without changing the hand of the fabric. Check Amazon.com. You can get sets of markers and ink workstations that come with the Fantastix pens which are just like markers you dip in the ink. Awesome.

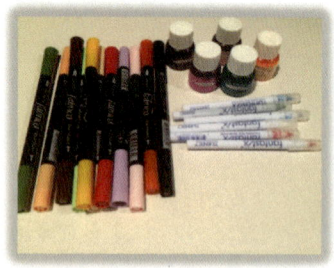

No water necessary. In fact, water can be bad on a quilt sandwich as it makes the inks run through to the back. Another one of those "ask me how I know" moments. Water is fine in cases when coloring the top only.

These products are color intense. For a lighter shade, drop a bit (smaller than a dime) of the ink onto disposable pallet paper or wax paper. Next to it, a drop of white and/or yellow. Also, squirt some generic aloe onto the paper. Take a toothpick or even with the marker tip, mix to get the color you want. You'll need a piece of the fabric you're using by your side to experiment. Please don't jump into your piece without knowing what color you're getting. I generally use the Fabrico markers to outline and add details.

After 24 hours of drying, heat set the inks with an iron for 15 seconds. Use a pressing cloth so you don't burn the fabric. Experiment with different paints and colored pencils, just make sure you wash your practice pieces. Not all surprises are good. See my YouTube channel for a demo on ink.

Finishing and Reflection

Looking at your piece even before you color it is exciting. All the different options you have to enhance it are wonderful, but can be overwhelming. There is no right or wrong, and frankly, you could leave it blank or wait to color it until you have more sections added around your quilt. You can reuse your freezer paper design over and over and try a few different options. I can't think of a better way to practice free motion quilting.

Once you're happy with your center section, trim it to 17.5" square, which it will probably be anyway. You'll always experience a bit of shrinking with the quilting, but what's nice about this method is that you can somewhat keep it under control as it's minimal with small sections.

This becomes the main piece which will grow as you add your sections and will be referred to as the MP. From here on out, you will be adding each section in a log cabin pattern. A traditional log cabin block is where you take a center square and add strips of fabric to the growing edges around it in either a clockwise or counter-clockwise direction. It can be as large as you want because you start in the center and work out. We're taking that block construction and using it for the layout of the entire quilt. This is the best way to learn the Quilt As *Inspired* approach as we can play with different techniques and free motion quilting stitches without worrying about matching anything to anything. It is my absolute favorite way to play with textiles and make a quilt. I sincerely hope you love it too.

SECTION 2:
HAND-BASTED, HAND-STITCHED APPLIQUE.

Materials For Section 2:

Two different background fabrics: Choose fabrics that will tie in some colors used in the first section. I used my inspiration print (3.25"x18") as well as a polka dot background (5"x18") for the applique.
Fabrics for applique: Use bits of fabrics for the petals and dots that contrast well with the background.
Backing fabric and Batting: Cut each into 19"x9" pieces.
Paper for given templates on p.22: Regular copy paper is just fine for this.
Starch/Best Press, Pressing Cloth and Iron: I typically use steam.
Thread and hand sewing needle: My favorite hand stitch needle is John James GoldNGlide Applique size 11. You can also use Milliners or Sharps. Experiment to see what you like.
Applique pins or Water based glue: To hold the applique in place while you hand stitch.
Blue Painter's Tape: You'll see I use the tape in different ways all the time. I buy ¼", ½" and 1" mostly.

Step 1: Make the Background.

Sew the long sides of the polka dot or chosen background fabric (5"x18") and the inspiration print (3.25"x18") together. The piece will measure 18x7.75" – the 18" is to allow for a bit of shrinkage during the quilting. NOTE: the background fabric that will hold the applique flowers is a bit short, so rather than having symmetrical 6" flowers, the 3" petals will be arranged to form a shorter blossom to fit onto the 5" background. See mine above.

Make your quilt sandwich and pin the corners. Don't baste until you read Step 2. We are going to quilt this before adding the applique and we need to plan for joining it to the MP.

Step 2: Planning to Join.

All sides can be quilted in any way you'd like all the way out to the edges except for one. The side you'll be attaching to the center section cannot have any quilting within ½" from the raw edge. You will still be using a ¼" seam allowance to join it after the quilting, but you'll need that additional space to trim the extra batting and fold over the backing to hand stitch in place (shown later in the joining).

Since you won't be doing any major quilting on the inspiration print, that becomes the logical joining side. Place a piece of blue painters tape covering ½" of that long edge as a reminder to stay away! See below:

With a walking foot, baste the opposite long edge with a 1/8" seam allowance. Don't worry about the short ends.

Step 3: The Quilting.

With your walking foot still attached and size 75 quilting needle, use a coordinating thread to ditch the seam joining the two fabrics. Remember that the bobbin thread will always need to be changed so the color matches the top thread. You could choose a wavy line from the decorative stitches on your machine and work a pass between the colors of the border print. That's all the quilting needed on the inspiration fabric.

For the pattern behind the applique, I chose a peachy rayon thread matching the background of the polka dot. I didn't want to add any complexity to the background so I kept it simple. Use your free motion foot to work a repetitive stem leaf pattern across just the polka dot section in one thread with no starts or stops.

Practice on Paper.

Practice doodling this or your chosen quilting design on paper or your iPad in Sketchbook Pro without lifting your pen. I started at lower right. Note the directional arrows. I stitched each leaf shape by traveling up the center vine and then branching out to the top of the leaf and then completing the bottom of the leaf back to the vine. First the right leaf and then the left. Then travel farther up the spine to the next set of leaves above. You can piggyback on basting and ditch lines to travel between vines. You don't need to mark the leaves. Draw the stem lines in chalk if you're afraid of veering off. See my YouTube channel for a demonstration of this quilting motif.

You can remove the tape, but don't trim the block just yet. There is a specific way to trim the joining edge that will be discussed in the joining section later. Leave the basting stitches on the opposite side intact. They'll be hidden in the ¼" seam later.

Orange Peel Template:

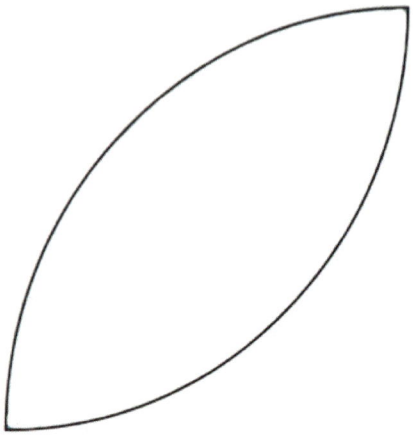

Orange peel block:

In traditional quilting, the orange peel block is a four-patch block made with curved piecing where you would put the four petal blocks together to make one adorable simple flower. If you Google "orange peel quilt block" you'll see some really great quilts made with just this one block.

In our case (as well as many quilters of today), we're going to use this template as an applique piece, turn the edges and then stitch it to the block. There are many different ways we can accomplish this, and if you already have a favorite – do it! Throughout the book I'll be showing different ways to work applique so you can learn them and choose your favorite. Many times, I choose the method by my mood and/or whether I need a take and go project if I'm out and about.

You'll need 12 templates as you'll be making three 4-petal flowers. Trace the design four times onto copy paper with a Sharpie (true to size at close to 3" from tip to tip) and run through your printer/copier 3 times to make 12 copies. Save the original. Cut them all out directly on the line.

Step 4: Applique Templates.

With a Frixion pen, trace the templates on the back of the chosen applique fabric 12 times. Leave enough room in between them so you can allow an approximate 1/3" cutting line around **each** piece. It is best to trace the templates on the bias so turning the curved edges is easier. Cut them out with seam as shown. Then pin one applique template to the WS of each cut-out shape within the line for turning. You can pin all of the templates to the fabric first and then cut them all out after as well. Whatever makes sense to you. I find cutting out the shapes without the papers pinned in place is easier.

NOTE: Your templates will be white – I printed different color templates first then removed the template color later for easier printing or copying from the book.

Step 5: Stitching and Turning.

Because the template piece is simple, you can hand baste the edges with needle and thread and then press them flat using heat and starch or Best Press. Thread a needle with a single thread and knot at end.

Starting at the middle of a long side, fold down seam at template edge, and using a needle and thread begin to baste large stitches to hold the edges in place. When you reach the tip, you'll be folding down one side, then overlapping the other to cover it. In the second picture, you'll see that it still extends beyond the template. Fold it back a third time and sew in place as shown in second picture.

Continue smoothing edges around template and sewing in place until the entire template is covered and looks like the photo on the previous page. Repeat for all 12 petals. Set aside while you do the circles.

Step 6: Perfect Circles.

I use Karen Kay Buckley's Perfect Circle templates. They are laser cut circles that come 4 each of many sizes. I highly recommend these if you're going to pursue applique. Until then, draw circles of chosen size on cardstock or no-melt Mylar template plastic. You can even use coins or washers. But careful. They're hot!

Trace circle template to the WS of the fabric, cut it out with a ¼" seam, then with a single strand of sewing thread do a basting stitch 1/8" away from raw edge. Place your template in the center and pull the thread to gather the stitches (below). Sew a few more stitches ½" or so beyond the beginning and clip the thread leaving a 4 inch tail.

Make four 1" circles to place in between the flowers and 3 ½" circles for the flower centers. See next page for setting, then removing templates.

Step 7: Trim the Block!

Once your piece is quilted, trim it up as follows: Square up the basted non-joining long side first. Then go ahead and trim the sides so that the piece measures 17.5" to match the main piece. **The joining side can now be squared up but YOU HAVE TO LEAVE AN EXTRA ¼ OF BATTING AND BACKING EXTENDING BEYOND THE RAW EDGE OF THE TOP LAYER. Lay your ruler so that the ¼" marking lies on the raw edge of the top layer then trim. You'll then have a bit of backing and batting extending beyond the top layer.**

This is so you can join the top layer with a ¼" seam and have enough extending to trim the batting and fold over and hand stitch the back to finish it up. More on this in the joining.

Step 8: Starch, Press and Arrange.

You can use any sizing or starch you want. My favorite product for this is Mary Ellen's Best Press because the fragrance is wonderful. It just makes me happy. Lay the pieces, around 4 at a time, WS up on your pressing surface and give them a squirt or two. Wait about 10 seconds for the starch to set in and then press with a hot iron for about 5-10 seconds. Then flip each one over and press again. Set aside to cool and do the rest of the shapes in batches.

For the petal templates turned with paper, gently clip all the basting threads away and remove the paper templates. The edges will stay turned so that stitching is easy. I usually press again after paper removal.

For the circles don't remove the stitching as you can't see the threads from the front. Rather, gently open the seam just barely enough on the right side of the 4" tail to slide the template out and then pull the tail thread gently so the circle retains its shape.

Center the pieces onto the background by pinning or using a few dots of water soluble glue on the seam allowances (not corners) of each piece so you can relax and stitch. Start with the center flower and work out from there. Keep at least ¼" space on the raw edge side of the background so the petals don't get cut off when adding another section. I left ½" just in case.

Step 9: Hand Stitch Applique.

Hand applique is one of my favorite things to do. It's so relaxing and you'll get a clean, crisp result.

Use a 24" single strand of silk or thin cotton thread that matches the applique (never the background) and knot at the opposite end of the needle. I used Aurafil thread.

Start by exiting the needle out of the folded edge of the applique piece. Insert the needle into the background fabric and batting (not back) directly under its exit point and come up 1/8" away catching the background and the very edge of the applique piece as shown above. Continue around the entire piece and knot at beginning. Weave tail into the batting, snugging up to hide the knot. See my Youtube video for additional guidance.

Repeat for all the pieces. If you wish, you can adorn the applique further by outlining each piece and/or adding extra decorative stitches on top of the applique. I've decided to leave well enough alone as I'm happy with it as is.

Step 10: The Joining!

It's finally time to attach this section to the main piece. This is the whole underlying basis for this method of quilt making. There is a set of guidelines to follow, but it's really very simple.

Take your trimmed (the joining side must have that extra ¼" of batting and backing extending past the top layer) and appliqued Section 2 and flip over so the back and batting can be folded back and you can match ONLY the top layer to any side of Section 1 right sides together:

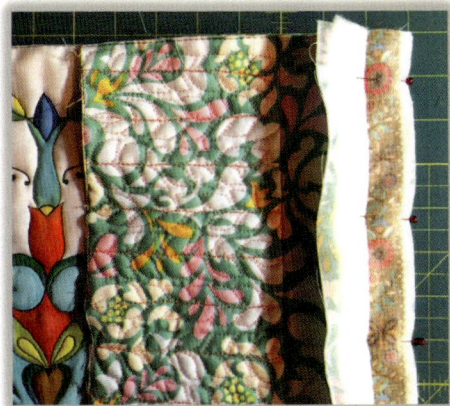 

Pin in place and sew together using a walking foot and a ¼" seam allowance. Remove pins and open up the quilt so it lays flat and the WS is facing up. Fold back the backing fabric, pin it out of the way and trim the extra batting. The batting that you're trimming should butt up with the batting within the seam that you just sewed. See above.

Run your iron across that new seam, matching battings and pressing into place. Take out the pins and press the backing fabric flat to cover all the raw edges. Then fold the raw edge of that backing fabric under so that the fold extends just barely beyond the new seam line. Press and hand stitch in place with the applique stitch spacing the stitches ¼" apart. After stitching in place, press both back and front. Trim and square up the MP which now measures approx. 17.5x24.5."

Yay! You've just begun your "Quilt As *Inspired*" journey! And I know what you might be thinking. Yes, you should hand stitch the backing fabric down after every section. It doesn't take long and it's good relaxing down time. This hand stitching time helps with the backlog of my Audible library and binge watching. Plus, by now, I'm tired and achy from sitting at my machine.

Section 3:
Wool Applique And Embroidery.

> **Materials For Section 3:**
>
> **Wool felt or Cotton for background 4.5"x25":** Using wool in the quilt adds great texture and gives the look of the traditional art of embroidered raw edge wool applique. It is fine to use cotton if wool isn't your favorite.
>
> **Scraps of wool felt and cotton for applique:** Wool is great because the edges don't need to be turned. Typically a blanket or buttonhole stitch is used to cover the edges and attach the pieces to the background. Of course, mixing and matching is always encouraged, so if you want to use a cotton background and apply wool applique to it or vice versa, that is wonderful. It's your quilt.
>
> **Backing Fabric and cotton flannel or bat 5.5"x26":** Use cotton flannel for batting with wool top.
>
> **Embroidery flosses and threads:** Anything goes here. I used DMC floss size 5, 2 plies of 6ply cross stitch threads, Perle cotton size 8 and 12 to embellish and add additional color and texture to the piece.
>
> **Given Templates (or your own). Tools for turning:** Apliquick tools or an orange stick or Hera marker.
>
> **Water Soluble Glue Stick:** Apliquick and Sewline are the best quilting glue sticks.
>
> **Fusible Web for cotton applique:** I use the Apliquick brand but there are others out there. Ask your LQS for a soft, lightweight fusible web that stays in the applique after the edges are turned.

Step 1: Make a Background.

I pieced a background with aqua and ochre. This decision was based on the fact that I didn't have a long enough piece of any one color of wool to cover the next side of the MP. I think it gives a little something extra. A lack of a material can easily turn into a design opportunity. The seams were pressed open to eliminate bulk. Make the quilt sandwich with chosen bat.

Step 2: Quick Quilting

Rather than free motion quilt, I decided to use some of my machine's decorative stitches in long lines to stabilize the piece. Remember to leave ½" untouched along the joining side. I only ran 4 lines of stitching along the length of the piece as I didn't want it to be too dense and I knew I was going to cover it with applique and embroidery.

NOTE: When selecting decorative stitches for quilting on wool, go simple. Even linear lines with a walking foot would be effective. Designs that work back and forth stitching, won't travel evenly on heavy fabrics. Just so you know, some of my applique pieces (the birds) are strategically placed to cover a few of my issues because I forgot that rule. Always practice. Shame on me.

Step 3: Attach it to the MP.

Now that it's quilted, you could join it to the MP before adding the details. Visually, it's easier to place threads and applique shapes based on what you've done already if it's attached. Of course, it's always more pleasant to stitch on a smaller section of fabric so the choice is yours.

Join this section in the exact same way as piece 2 was added. I'll refer you to page 25 when we join in this way. I want to fill the pages with new information rather than repeat the joining instructions after each section. Soon you won't have to look them up. You'll remember how through practice. Below is a photo of the applique stitch used to close up the seam in the back.

Trim and square it up. My piece measures 21.25"x24.25" It's okay if yours isn't the same. In log cabin, any size goes. You can trim to make it match mine now or just know going forward that the measurements I'll give in the materials lists will have to be adjusted for the size of your MP.

Step 4: Adorn.

There are so many different ways to decorate this new addition to your quilt. Of course, you can certainly copy what I did and I'll give you instructions for that, but if something else pops into your head and you want to try it, please do. All of the applique and hand stitching can be done without working all the way through to the back. Just stitch it all through the top and batting. Hide your knots behind the applique pieces.

Put a bird on it! And leaves and flowers, etc…Start with templates. Draw your own, search online or you can use the ones on the next page that I traced and enlarged of simplified images from a Dover Scandinavian coloring book. These books are invaluable for design inspiration and are copyright free.

Get these through Amazon.com where I get everything I can't find locally. There are hundreds to choose from. I rarely color in mine. Instead, I use the designs for quilting lines and applique shapes. That way I can color them over and over again on fabric!

Left is a wool bird, a wool heart, a larger heart cut from fusible template and the cotton I'm going to use for the cotton applique under the wool heart. See next pages for all the steps.

Hand Drawn Templates:
Below are the outlines of the exact templates I used. They are true to size. Just copy this page or trace the shapes. Cut them out on the line, trace them on chosen wool fabric, and cut directly on line. Details are worked in the stitching.

Practical Embroidery Practice

1. You'll find basic embroidery stitches here and on the next page to work through. And as long as we're practicing embroidery, we may as well make something beautiful. This could be the center block of your next quilt! Start with a 13" square of dark grey cotton and hoop it.

2. Pop a **French knot** in the center: Thread a length of #8 Perle cotton and tie a knot. Pull up at the center cross from behind the work. Hold the thread out with your left hand and point the needle downward. Wind the thread around the needle 4 times. The secret to the French knot is to take your left hand thread and swing it under the needle and hold it taut before you insert the needle back into the fabric just a few threads away from the start. Lefties reverse the hands.

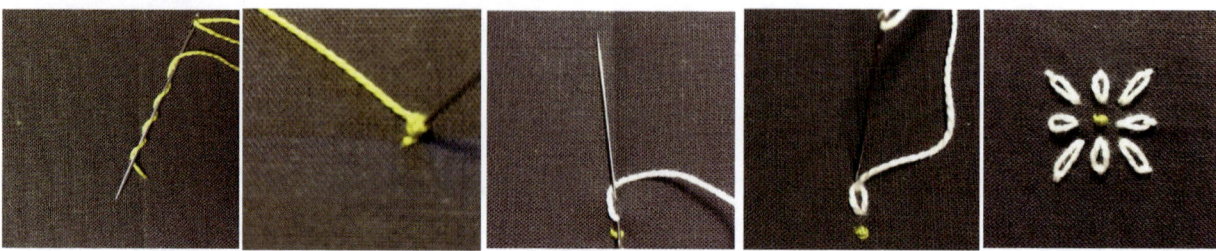

3. Next do some long and short **Lazy Daisy** stitches around the knot in white. Thread your needle, and come up about 1/8" away from the knot on the straight line. Insert the needle into the exact same spot and then exit 1/8" away from the start up that line. Wrap the thread under the needle and pull through. Insert the needle on the outside of the top of the loop and pull under. Make 3 more short ones at the bottom and sides. Then in between them, do long stitches, coming up ¼" away.

4. You can add shapes with the **Back Stitch.** With a chalk pencil, draw lines North and South connecting two long daisies. Thread a needle with red and knot at the other end. Come up 1/8" from where you want the line to start. Insert the needle into the start point and come up 1/8" after the starting line. Pull through. Keep stitching in this way to cover your drawn line. At the point, exit the needle right out of the tip of the point from underneath and insert the needle in the spot you would have if you kept going straight. Then come up 1/8" away from the point down the next line. Finish other side. Work lazy daisy stitches and French knots to fill the shapes.

 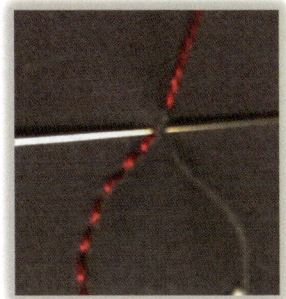 

5. Work some detail with **Stab or Straight Stitches,** which is the easiest of stitches as you just come up at the start point from behind and insert the needle at the end point. Fill the lazy daisy stitches and make a few stitches between the daisies. This stitch is used to make satin stitch fills which you will see lots of in Section 6.

6. Mark lines above and following the red shape stitch with the **Stem (Outline) Stitch.** Come up at the beginning of the line and insert the needle ¼" away and come up again right in the middle of the two points and pull through. Hold the thread to the same side of the line every time you repeat the stitch so that it always lies on one side. Each subsequent stitch will be worked at a slight diagonal and come up at the last insertion point. Keep the stitches short.

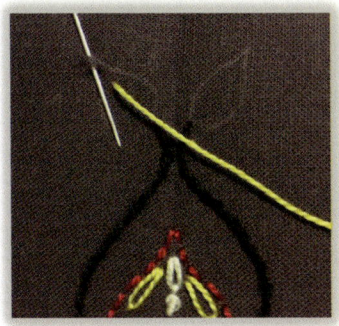 

7. Fill the leaf shapes with the **Fishbone Stitch.** Come up ¼" from the tip of the leaf from behind. Insert the needle at the tip of the leaf and come back up 1/8" on the leaf line to the left and pull through. Insert needle on the center line just below the starting point and come up on the right outer leaf line parallel to the top of the left line you made previously. Pull through. Continue inserting the needle into the center line and coming up on the drawn line alternating sides.

8. The **Feather Stitch (like fly)** is perfect for freeform stems to add other stitches to. Start from the top and work downward. Come up at the point where the top of the stem will be from behind. Insert the needle to the right and across from the starting point and insert needle ½" below and in the center of both. Wrap thread under the needle and pull through. Alternate the stitches back and forth working downward on a vertical center stem. Make it a combo platter and mix it up!

Step 5: Glue-Turned Applique.

A Starch Alternative.

Rather than using heat and starch to turn as we did in section 2, here you'll learn to use a stay-in fusible interfacing and water-soluble glue. Use this when not stacking layers of applique on top of each other as the extra bulk under one layer doesn't affect the hand of the quilt much. If you have a multi-layer applique shape, stick with the removable templates or freezer paper. More details on this in future Sections.

Draw the shape on the shiny side of the fusible and cut it out on the line in the exact size as your template with no seam allowance.

Fuse the shape for a few seconds with a dry iron to a carefully selected place (if you want a fussy cut applique) on the WS of your chosen fabric. Make sure shiny side is on fabric. You don't want that on your iron! Let it cool.

Cut the shape out of the fabric with a ¼" seam allowance for turning. This product is meant to stay in the applique and will gradually soften over time.

As a general rule, you'll want to clip any valleys in the shape for easier turning. Note how I cut a slit in the "V" about a thread away from the fusible. I also cut across the point rather than keeping it sharp to eliminate bulk.

Turn it Under:

Start turning on a straight edge or a point rather than a curve. Work 4-6 inches at a time. The glue dries fast in dry climates. Always keep the cap on.

Run a line of glue from the point and around to the V of the heart. Begin at the point and press the fabric down along the edge of the fusible.

When turning around a curve, take tiny pressing movements along the folding line, rather than pressing from the raw edges of the fabric. If you get points, fix them with the sharp end of your cuticle stick or tools. If you work relatively quickly, the glue is repositionable. Keep working the other side down to the point.

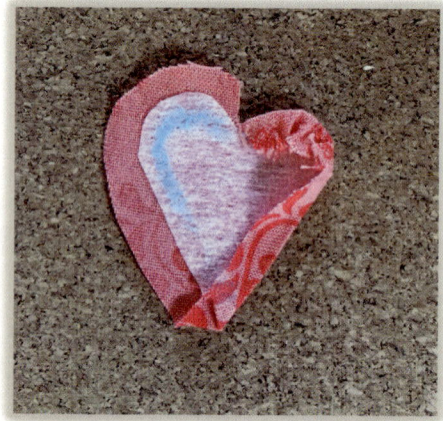

Voila! Ready to stitch down.

For a demo, see my Youtube video on this.

30

Step 6: Embroider.

I embroidered the bird details and added the cotton tail feather piece before I added the birds to the background. The flower stem on their tummies is done with the outline (stem) stitch, the leaves are lazy daisy, the petals and tail details are open lazy daisy, eyes are backstitch and extended French knots, and the tail has straight (stab) stitches for joining to the bird and for textured detail.

Wool applique pieces can easily be added to a background using the blanket (or buttonhole) stitch around the piece. Once you get going, it's very easy, but starting is sometimes the hard part (as with anything, am I right?)

Shown at right, I am using 2 strands of the 6 strand DMC embroidery floss normally used for cross stitch. Cut a length of about 24" and knot the end. Hide the knot in the wool under applique and exit the needle just at the side of your piece. Insert the needle into the applique about 1/8" to the left and in from the edge of the exit point (or right if you're left handed) and exit out of background directly adjacent and OVER the working thread as shown. Practice!

I used the stem and feather stitch for the blue flower stem, reverse blanket stitches around flower, feather stitches for sprays coming out of the flower. I then added a few French knots and one to hold down a tiny wool circle. Stem stitch to outline the white cotton piece, lazy daisies under and around the round flower. Stab stitches in the flower. Cross stitches and backstitch to add details to background. I really enjoy using different materials to achieve the details in embroidery. The juxtaposition between the sheen of silks and cottons and matte of wool makes for a very interesting piece. Use different size threads to add further interest. Collect threads and flosses when you're out and about - you never know when you'll need that perfect bit of thread.

There is a great variety of more complicated embroidery stitches out there, and I encourage you to learn all that you can because it is the most relaxing artform I have found to date. Ok, second to knitting. But in reality, the stitches shown on the previous pages are all you need to make really spectacular pieces. Using different colors, textures and materials like silk, wool and cotton, and stacking and mixing the stitches, you can create magic!

Visit my Youtube channel on embroidery to watch a video for more guidance.

SECTION 4:
FAIR ISLE STRIPS

This 6-fabric section is fairly easy and goes pretty fast. I used different contrasting colors to resemble some of the repetitive knitting that I absolutely love from Scandinavia. I looked through my stash and found a plaid and a couple of stripy "fair isle" type fabrics that I thought would work well with the main piece. In the spirit of folk art living, using what I have makes me really happy. The orange and aqua section is the only pieced part of the section with 14 alternating 2" squares.

Materials for Section 4:

6 Fabrics: These may need to be pieced together if using fat quarters. Just watch the repeat and try to match the design up when joining: (1) A small-print repetitive fabric that measures 22"x2.5"; (2) a fat quarter each of orange and teal dot for the pieced zigzag section that will measure 22x2" (instructions to follow); (3) 22x¾" strip of solid yellow; (4) 22x1" strip of teal; (5) 22x1.5" strip of plaid; (6) 22x3.25" strip of long stripe fabric.
Backing fabric and batting: 9"x23" of each
Painter's Tape, Frixion Pen and Transparency Sheet.
Thread for Quilting: I used Mettler silk finished cotton.

Step 1: The Pieced Section.
Cut 14 2" squares for zigzag color (aqua).
Cut 28 1.5" squares for background (orange).

Flip each background square over so WS is facing you, and with a Frixion pen, draw a diagonal line from corner to corner and then an additional line ½" away for bonus mini half square triangles to be used in another project. Place a small marked square on the upper right corner of each larger square and chain piece as shown below. Stitch directly on each larger line first and then start again at the top and sew the smaller line.

Cut between the sewn lines so each smaller end triangle comes off. You'll get cute little squares (shown at the right) sewn and ready to use at another time. Set aside.

 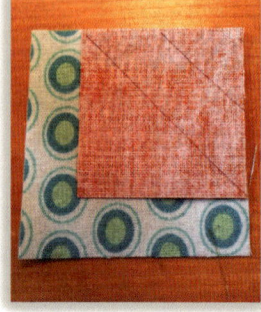 

Step 1: continued…

Open up the flap of each larger square and press seam to the background color.

Repeat this entire process at the opposite corner for each of the 14 squares. Press all seams towards background. Square up to 2." Sew the squares together in one long strip so the line forms a zig zag.

Step 2: Strip Piece the Rest

Sew the long edges of all the fabric strips together in the order listed under Materials for Section 4. When all sewn together, the strata (strip set) will measure 22"x~8.5." Make your quilt sandwich and mark off the ½" of the joining edge (1st fabric listed) with painter's tape.

Step 3: The Quilting.

I envisioned each section to have its own pattern that runs across the entire length of itself to complement the idea of fair isle patterning. One of my favorite ways to experiment with different quilting patterns is to place a piece of transparency or clear film over the section of the quilt and tape in place. Grab a Sharpie marker and start playing. This also counts as "doodling it first" and will embed it into your head and hand. Here's my initial drawing:

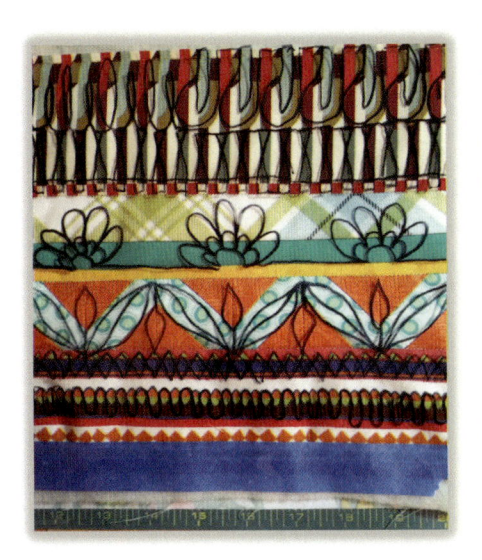

I ditch stitched each seam with my walking foot and thin cotton thread to secure. It makes all the difference.

*The bottom section has three simple lines of quilting. The U-shaped line was done with one thread. The diagonals took two rows of zigzagging.

*The pieced section was done with one thread.

*The solid/plaid section was done with one thread.

*The long stripes I did in two sections. The first being long and short loops and then shorter loops from the top.

My quilting doesn't look exactly like the picture, but it's okay because I got a good idea of what my initial vision will look like. I decided to simplify the long stripy section. As you can see from the previous page, I chose one lighter quilting thread to blend in with the piece.

Trim it up starting with the long side opposite the joining side and then the two short sides. Don't forget to leave that extra ¼" of batting and backing extending beyond the top. Refer to page 25 for the detailed review on joining. Square the MP up. My piece measures 32.25x21.25"

Here we are! At the time of this writing, this is as far as my quilt has gotten. We are building this together!

SECTION 5:
PATCHWORK AND PAINTING

This is a Frayed Sawtooth Frame block which includes flying geese units and four patches. The block will finish at 8." The picture below is shown at 6.5" to fit the page. If you'd rather make templates than rotary cut, enlarge this image until the outside square measures 8". Each line of the pattern would be the **sewing line** so with a Frixion pen, draw the line on the WS of the fabric and cut with a ¼" seam allowance. Sew along the drawn line.

If not making templates, rotary cutting instructions are next.

Materials for Section 5:

Fabrics: A fat quarter each of white, red, apple green, teal, aqua (of course you can do whatever colors you want, just refer to mine for placement of the patches).
Backing fabric and Wool batting 34"x10"
Backing fabric 1"x32.5": For the back sashing as we will be joining with sashing this time.
Sashing fabric 1.5x32.5": I used a graphic black and white print folded to make little triangles.
Inks or Motif Fabric: Same inks as Section 1, or if fussy cutting, look for a fabric that has 4" motifs or smaller.
Threads: Black Rayon, Mettler in Red and Aqua.
Original Freezer Paper Drawing, Frixion Pen, Lightbox

When I decide on a block, I like to color it first to decide if it's going to work. You can copy the block diagram on the next page (if you have a copier with a lid or draw the lines with a straightedge and Sharpie and run a few copies through your inkjet printer) and do the same until you get it the way you want it. Even then, I make one block first just to make sure I'm in love. If so, I'll chain piece the rest of them in assembly line style. With chain piecing, it all goes fast. The cutting instructions on the next page are for one square, but you'll make four ultimately.

I left the center square white, as I plan to bring a motif from Section 1 into these units. If you will be doing the same thing, find a motif from your original freezer paper drawing that fits well within a 4" square and transfer the design BEFORE making your sandwich. I pieced all the blocks, stitched them together to form the entire section and then transferred the design following the steps in Section 1. The other option is to fussy cut something fabulous out of a coordinating fabric.

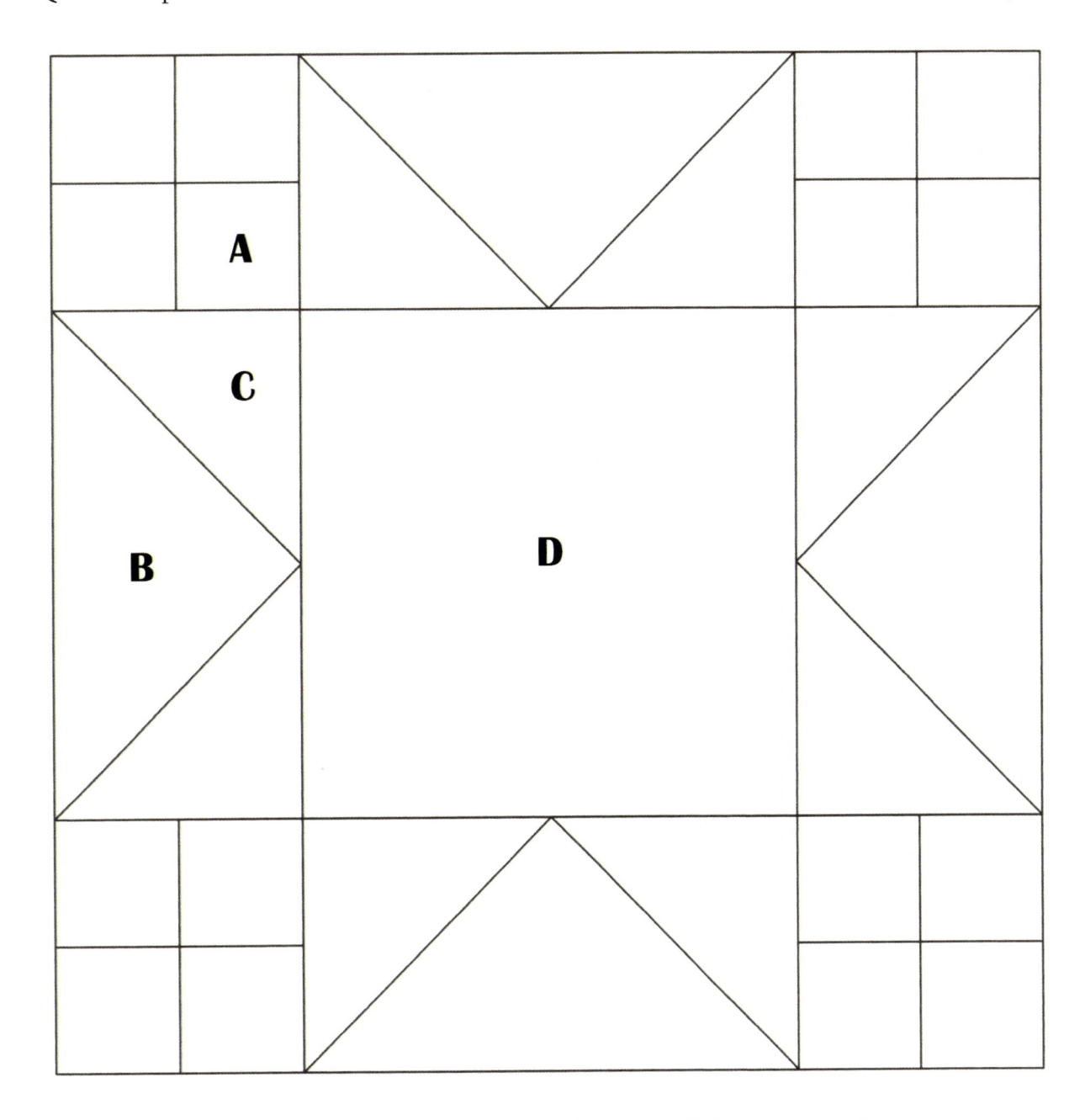

Cutting instructions:

Patch A: cut eight 1 ½" squares EACH of two colors (where I have red and green)
Patch B: cut one 5 3/16" square, and then cut twice diagonally (where I have teal)
Patch C: cut four 2 7/8" squares, and then cut once diagonally (where I have aqua)
Patch D: cut one 4 ½" square.

Obviously, we are working in very small fractions so accuracy is key. Measure twice. Cut once. When I see a 16th inch measurement, I have been known to round up to the nearest eighth and then trim down. Just make sure you are trimming and squaring up the block from the center and not cutting too much off one side of the unit.

Hint: I like to put each newly cut patch on its corresponding space in the block like working a puzzle to make sure I have what I need. Remember, they will be larger as the cut measurements above include a ¼" seam allowance and this block diagram is 6.5" instead of our 8" finished block.

Step 1: Flying Geese.

Assemble the flying geese units. Make four per block. If you've done any quilting, you've probably worked with these. Seemingly simple, they can be tricky. Here are hints:

Line up a long side of Patch C with a short side of Patch B. There is a bit of extra fabric on Patch C that will extend beyond the point of the tip of Patch B as shown:

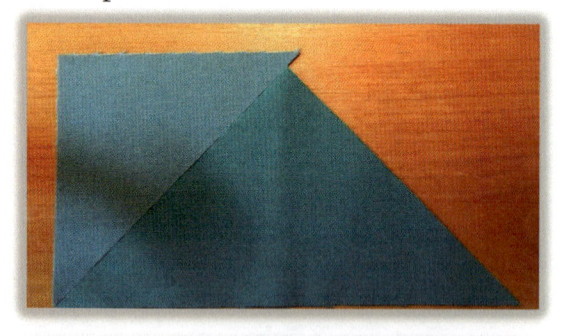

Flip patch C over so right sides are together and bottom edges match. Sew ¼" seam. Press seam towards "wing"

Place second Patch C along the other side of B and stitch. Press seam to "wing." Be sure to have ¼" at top above tip or it will get cut off when you sew it to the block. Each unit measures 2.5"x4.5" Clip those dog ears.

There are wonderful flying geese rulers and modern methods to make these easier and faster. They are great, but I'm a purist. It's best to know how to make the basic goose unit first so you understand what it is you are making easier. Sometimes I look through all my extra rulers and forget what they're for.

Step 2: Four Patches.

These are the most basic blocks of all. And when you chain piece them, they go fast. Place 2 opposite color squares together RS facing and sew all together with a ¼" seam.

Chain piecing is the best way to go about this. You won't be cutting threads between the little blocks each time. Just keep feeding them in one right after the other. Leaving needle in the down position and stitching a few stitches between blocks saves on thread and gives you a better chance of keeping your fabric from getting caught in the throat plate.

When they're all sewn, clip the threads between each block and press the seam towards the dark fabric. Now you can place the two patches together lining up opposite colors and snuggle the seams that lie opposite each other as shown:

Place a pin in the seam if it makes you feel safe – I don't on things this small. Remove pins just before they enter the needle. Pins can possibly distort the sewing line. You can chain piece these as well. Press seam open. Measures 2.5x2.5" Perfect patchwork!

Trim the blocks to the size indicated as needed. It's much nicer to work with straight edges. I use steam in the iron because I like my pieces flat. I do use Best Press quite a bit especially on small patchwork so fabric doesn't feel floppy. Plus there's that comforting homey aroma.

Step 3: Assemble the Block.

Time to put this block together! Put the rows together first. Start with the middle section and sew a flying geese unit to either side – being careful to point the tip of the goose towards the middle as shown on the diagram. You want a ¼" seam allowance, as always, but more importantly, the sewing line needs to cross just on the inside of the seam allowance so the tip doesn't get cut off. If you have less of a ¼" from tip of goose to edge, place that goose so the fabric underneath is showing:

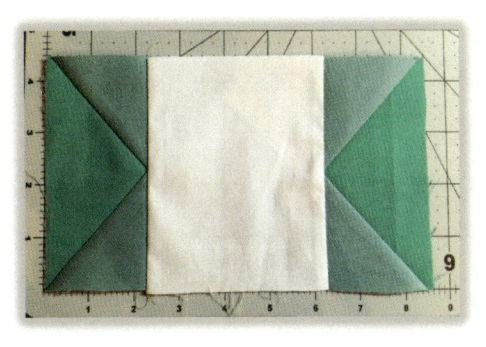

Oh my gosh! My needle holder is super dusty. Don't forget to clean out the bobbin and needle area. The general rule is every bobbin change, take your brush and clean it out! I try.

Square it up. The unit should measure 4.5"x8.5" My tips are within 1mm so I'm happy. If your tips are more cut off than you want, it's ok to take out the seam and do it again. The only way to become an amazing accurate piecer is if you are willing to redo it over and over until it is perfect. That takes the joy right out of quilting for me, so I have lower standards. I do my best work and sleep well at night. No Stepford people here.

Stitch the remaining four patches to either side of the other two geese units. Be mindful of the four patch line up when the blocks are placed together. You can do a checkerboard or a mirror image. Play around with them and you'll see what I mean. As you can see from photos below, I did checkerboard for the two sides, but when they meet in the middle, the checkerboard goes the opposite way. This makes for mirror image quilting motifs. But remember – there is no right and wrong. Now sew the rows together – again being mindful that the tips of the geese point to center.

Place your block up next to your quilt to make sure you like it. If it's off, don't be afraid to change out the colors or even try a different 8" block (8.5" unfinished). In this case, I really love the way the colors of the new block pull in the rest of the quilt. My eye travels well enough around the piece and seems to complement the Fair Isle section. I made 3 more blocks and stitched them together.

You will be joining this to the quilt with a border sashing. You also might be noticing that these blocks seem huge next to the smaller intricate sections of the quilt so far. "So far" is the key phrase. We have a long way to go. It will balance out as we add more large blocks around!

Keep the faith and the grand scheme of the quilt in perspective. Just keep going. I always question the first few sections until I get twice around. You might be wondering when is it finished? Stop when you've had enough and are happy with the piece. All it will just need at any point you decide it's completed is a binding and label.
And a sleeve, if you'll be hanging it.

Step 4: the Quilting.

My favorite part. But even still, I usually have to stare at it until an idea pops up. And it always does. Eventually. Then I draw the idea out and stitch it. Most of the time, I'm happy with the result. Sure, there are times when I wish I would have used a different thread or pattern, but rarely do I tear out quilting. Those are learning opportunities for next time. I like to call that experience. If you're using motifs from Section 1, trace them now and then make your quilt sandwich. This strip should measure 8.5"x32.5" I used pins at the corners and long sides and didn't baste since we're ditching.

I already know that I'm going to quilt the middle section of each block with a motif from Section 1 in black thread. But I don't want to use black for the whole section as I have used multiple colors throughout the quilt and want to be consistent in that regard. Before that happens, you need to secure this section by ditching with a walking foot and clear thread. It will accomplish two things. First, running a stitching line around the major seams will help avoid the sandwich from slipping and sliding around while you do the decorative stitches. And just importantly, as you move the section under your machine, you become more comfortable with the piece and ideas sometimes appear out of nowhere. Plus it feels really good and puffy and quiltalicious. Don't skip the ditching and use your walking foot as it's more accurate. Since we're joining with sashing, you can quilt all the way out to the edges on all sides. Remove pins.

Above is what mine looks like with the sections ditched and the motif done. Note that I didn't run a quilt line down the middle teal diamonds or the lines within each 4 patch – I wanted them to appear as their own unit so I left them alone.

I used a teal thread to quilt detail in the lighter sections where I decided to do pebbles outside a curvy line to outline the teal block. I did this in one single thread starting at the right upper side triangle and was able to carry the design to the next section at each corner. I worked counterclockwise around the entire piece. Other than the motif taken from my original freezer paper design, I did not do any marking.

Pebbles can bring wonderful texture to a piece. Practice these before you work on your quilt, but basically, just work a lot of circles of various sizes and figure 8s that lie right next to each other. Working different size circles and going over the lines more than once will add interest to the piece. See my YouTube demo on this. For the four-patch sections, I added a leaf shape on the green in its complimentary color (red) to mimic a part of the motif I decided on for the center.

Step 5: Trimming and Joining with Sashing:

This is a great way to add a section without having to worry about leaving that ½" space on one side. It's a great option for adding a section that you want to quilt all the way to the edges. This method is also used when making a quilt with blocks that you might want to create some intricate stitching on before putting them all together. Oh say a Baltimore Album. Next on my list!

Line up Section 5 to its placement on the main piece side by side. As you can see, my section 5 ended up a bit shorter so I had to trim the quilt about 1/8" so that they are the same size. This may happen a bit more often as the sections get bigger. Set aside Section 5.

Fold the 1 ½" front sashing in half lengthwise WS together so you'll end up with a piece that's ¾" by the length of the section you're adding (here the sashing might be just a bit longer as the piece is now approximately 32" – you can trim it after joining. I fussy cut my sashing so that when folded, little black triangles run the length of the section.

Place the 1" backing strip RS up. On top of that, place main piece RS up so that the back fabrics are together. Lastly, place the folded front sashing on top of the main piece (fold to left). See order below left photo:

The photo above left just shows the order. You'll need to stack and line them so that all raw edges are together and facing to the right. Pin every 6 inches and use a walking foot to stitch the layers together with a ¼" seam as shown below. Take the pins out just before you get to them. Pins can really distort a seam line, particularly when the fabric layers are thick.

Step 6: Adding Section 5.

Turn the piece over and press the back strip up and away from the quilt. You'll be joining Section 5 to this piece **only** so leave the front sashing where it is. Don't try to press that open quite yet.

With the WS of the quilt still facing up, place Section 5 on top with the raw edges lined up and back fabrics together, being mindful of which way Section 5 will face the rest of the quilt when you open it up. I wanted my flowers to grow outward so I placed the section so that it looks upside down:

Align the raw edges and pin every 6 inches and stitch with a ¼" seam with your walking foot. Open it up and press the seams from the back first.

Flip the quilt so the RS is facing up and press the front sashing up towards the new section. The good news is, the back is completely done. The other news is that you still have to hand stitch the folded end of the front sashing down (applique stitch) to cover the newly sewn seam. While you're stitching, relax and be in the moment. Enjoy the slow repetitive motion and revel in the fact that you are making something beautiful with your hands.

The piece now measures 29.5"x31.75" after trimming and adding Section 5.

Section 6:
Dala-Floda Embroidery

There can't be anything more Scandinavian than Dala-Floda embroidery. This originated from the Dalarna region in Sweden and was used primarily in folk costumes. The bright bursts of flowers and leaves against a black or dark background is not only eye candy, but really fun to do. It may look overwhelming as a whole, but just like this method of quilt making, we're going to take it step by step. While I've been embroidering for some time, this is my first attempt at this style of stitching. I am confident that yours will be just as vibrant and wonderful. Don't get nervous that you are not seeing a whole pattern or template given for this section. I did this entire piece without any plan or specific patterns. I had only my own drawings, my trusty Scandinavian Designs color book, a few copyright free images off Google and a basket of colorful Paternayan Persian wool embroidery yarn. My best advice is to not worry about planning the whole thing out, just take one tiny step and begin your journey. It's a relaxing and scenic trip. If embroidery is not your thing, just find the same size piece of fabric that is packed with floral prints and use it instead.

Materials:

Black Fabric: 6"x35": Black cotton or wool felt. I used cotton this time.
Fusible Fleece: 6"x35" (if using cotton background). This is Pellon 987F. I go to the big box store and buy this on an unopened full bolt and use a 50% off one cut fabric coupon. A great deal. I use this product all the time.
Backing Fabric and Batting: 7"x35" and additional backing strip 1"x35"
White Fabric Strips: 1"x35" and 1.5"x35"
Paternayan or other Wool Embroidery Yarn, DMC floss, and/or embroidery threads.
Tapestry needles and Embroidery Hoop.

More on Materials.

The background traditionally was made with wool felt. Of course, you can use that like we did in Section 3. But this time, I used black cotton because I had it on hand and also I wanted to experiment with different materials. Plus my plan is to quilt the background after the embroidery, so I wanted to keep it a lighter piece.

The yarn used for the embroidery is called Paternayan. It's a 3-ply Persian wool yarn that comes in hundreds of colors. One 8-yard skein of each color is plenty, as you'll only be using one ply at a time, and I used around 20 different colors. You can get them online for less than $2 per skein. If you can't find it locally, jump online and grab some. It is readily available.

You may have some sport weight wool yarn on hand that you could try. I didn't have a bright red in Paternayan so I did use a sport weight knitting yarn for that color, but it frayed easily so I had to use shorter pieces. Best to use wool yarn specifically for embroidery/needlepoint.

Wool Alternates

I am always a fan of using what you have so if by now you're thinking about that bucket full of DMC floss you already own, I say try it! I've broken tradition by using cotton so what the heck – give it a shot. It may give you the look you want.

This embroidery style is most effective when you can do some shading. In other words for each color get a light, medium and dark value. I used 5 different greens, a white, 3 different yellows, 3 different blues, etc. you get the idea. Unfortunately, I can't share all the exact color numbers that I used because I had a stash of this yarn left over from a knitting project. It really doesn't matter – there are so many to choose from – make it your own! To scale down the options, steer clear of colors that are heathered or muted. To capture the spirit of Dala-Floda, use clear bright colors. A few pastels are okay for your lighter values.

Use a hoop for each section. Just do. The piece will shrink and be wobbly as you work, Hoops do help. I resisted the hoop for a long time and still only use it when I have to. I'm always afraid that the hoop will distort the work I've already done, but so far so good. I guess that is what they're made for. Go figure.

The Stitching.

I used a 12" hoop so only the sides were stabilized and pulled tight which was enough. Use a tapestry or embroidery needle that has a point sharp enough to pierce the cotton and an eye just large enough to hold one strand of the wool yarn. I have a variety pack of needles from John James specifically for embroidery and ribbon work so that I always have the needle I need. Experiment with a few brands and sizes to see what you love.

Seventy-five percent of the stitching in this section is done with satin stitch. This is basically working straight stitches (as shown on page 29) right next to each other to fill in a given shape. As you can see above, I varied the lengths of the darker green stitches so that the lighter green could be filled in and would better blend into each other. This is called, oddly enough, the blended satin stitch.

See my YouTube video on embroidery stitches, but basically you'll be working on the front of the piece with your needle held parallel to the background and making each stitch with one motion with the needle going in and out of the fabric at the same time like using a safety pin, rather than working up and then down in two needle moves. It will feel more like a whipstitch. To get nice clean edges on the outside of the shape, go down or come up (depending on which angle you're working) exactly on the drawn line. By the time you get to the end of the shape, the chalk line will be gone. Work firm enough to make a nice flat stitch, but don't pull too tight.

Pattern Transfers

I don't do a lot of whole design copy transferring as, frankly, I'm too lazy to go through the steps or get in the car and run to the copy place to blow up a design just so I can change it while I work (I tend to do that). There are lots of stencils and huge pattern pieces you can buy, and as many different ways to transfer a design to your fabric. But the prep work of transferring an entire design takes too long for me. My fingers itch to get to the stitching so, like the way I live my life, I stay in the moment and design while I go. This might sound a little scary. But give it a try. If you draw out a shape you don't like, erase it and try another. It's better than spending an entire day on copying over an enormous design where some elements may not fit anyway. Don't forget to doodle designs before bed or in the morning with your coffee. Or both. Get that right side of the brain working!

Step 1: The Setup.

Fuse the fleece to the backside of the cotton with a hot, steamy iron. If using wool, it will already be thick enough so the extra structure isn't needed. My piece didn't shrink much lengthwise, but ended up at 5.5" wide when I finished.

Draw a chalk line lengthwise down the center of the block and machine stitch a line. This will help with embroidery placement. Use either a straight line or a few choices from your machine's decorative stitches.

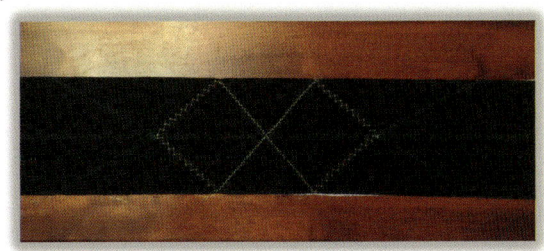

Mark the center, draw and stitch a few more lines at whatever angles you'd like. Here, I did 45 degree angles radiating out from the center and then for the outer lines, I marked each lengthwise edge 12" away from the middle and stitched a line from the center squiggle to those marks. Don't lament over the decision-making of thread colors and line shape. Most of it will get covered up. Again, these are mostly for guidelines to create your mirror image stitching.

Now what? Looking at this can be like an artist staring at a blank canvas scared stiff and wondering what the heck to paint. First of all. Relax. You cannot mess this up. It isn't supposed to look like anything so you can't fail. Go back in time to a childlike place and play. Get out your mandala color books or just start drawing some shapes on paper. It's funny, I naturally draw the same 5 shapes over and over so I have to force myself to find some new line to draw. It's good for me.

And for you. You will get better at this I promise. If you're at a loss, copy what I did and ideas will flow. It's the natural order of things. Keep an open mind and let your right brain take it. No rules. No fear. No problem.

Step 2: Begin the Stitching.

Remember Maria...Let's start at the very beginning. A very good place to start.

Have faith. Have fun. We are working mirror image designs, so starting right smack dab in the middle is best. While I didn't work with a full template, I wanted to get the mirror image shapes "close" to identical so I had a piece of paper and a Micron pen by my side. You don't need a Mircon pen of course, but they're awesome. If they ever stop making them, I'll die.

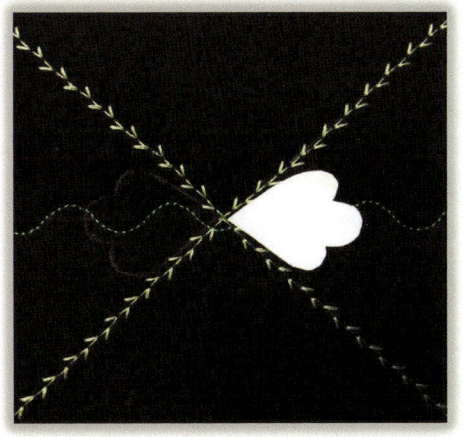

As you can see, I'm stitching as I draw the design. If you try to draw or transfer an entire design first, all the chalk will rub off. Which is annoying. Besides that, we don't even have an entire design. Instead, each design element will be dictated by the ones that were stitched before it. Go ahead and draw a shape like mine on paper, cut it out and trace it onto your background with chalk on each side of the center cross. These go on the center line pointing out to each long end.

Stitch it with blended satin.

The next series of photos show the continuation of the stitching. Again, I didn't have a plan for the entire piece, just a few photos and some paper to draw the templates I wanted to mirror.

The bright blue flowers are just a circle of lazy daisy stitches and an orange French knot center.
The second pic shows a satin stitch shape bordered with lazy daisy chains, and a center tie of red lazy daisies.
The last shows red scrolls started with stem stitch and turned into satin. And a chalk drawing of next shape.

By taking it one step at a time, mirroring each shape from top to bottom, and enjoying the slow stitching process, a design emerges that looks completely planned out. The traditional way to decorate a space with Dala-Floda (also known as sewn-on embroidery) is to start with a large flower or motif and then fill the space around it with leaves, vines and smaller flowers. I didn't focus so much on exactly mirroring the smaller components - close enough is good enough. Don't try to fill in the entire space with stitching. Negative space is important here. Also, if you're not sure what to do in the current section you're working, it's okay to move on to work something different and then come back and fill in details later.

For the fan flower, I used a paper template to draw the bottom heartish shapes and then drew the 6 petals freehand all at once so I could visualize the whole unit. I did have to redraw a few shapes as I stitched because the chalk lines disappear pretty quickly. I worked satin stitch for all the flower components and the darker green part of the leaf in photo 1. The gold part of the leaf I worked in blanket stitch. I free drew the leaf in the second pic and worked fly stitch in aqua. Even with the hoop, and not pulling too tight, you'll notice quite a bit of wrinkling, shrinking and pulling of the fabric. That's normal and ok. You will be ironing this flat and quilting the background later.

44

Quilt As Inspired   Ann Myhre

Here is the completed fan flower section. All the leaves I drew free hand with no template. If you look closely, you can see that the shapes are not identical. For me, that gives the piece that hand crafted, folk art charm. It's more important that you have a chalk line for big pieces to follow, than it is for all the smaller pieces match perfectly. Some leaves I did in satin, some in fly stitch and the vines in stem stitch. The different textures add interest and are more fun to look at. I utitlized the machine-sewn lines to center the small bud stemming from the flower.

Note that for the center section, I added backstitch gold scrolls, fly stitch leaves to connect the gold flowers, and the blossoms at each end I worked satin in 2 yellows and a white.

If you fold the whole piece in half and mark the placement of the top of the bud and the bottom of the hearts on the other side of the center stitching, you'll be assured that you stay *releatively* in line with the first fan flower unit you did.

But there's still a lot of real estate at the ends. Read on…

Starting a section is always the hardest. I went back to my trusty coloring book. I drew a few budding shapes with chalk.
Second photo shows the shapes filled in with yellows and golds and the beginnings of a flower center.
I filled the jagged shapes with satin stitch and drew 5 large petals, which I'll have to redraw periodically, which is okay.

The fun part! Petals in 3 colors of aqua blue. Satin Stitch in motion. But my chalk lines are disappearing! Time to redraw. Finished Petals in the second photo. I must say it's gorgeous. Couldn't have come out better even with a proper transfer. A couple of leaves, drawn and stitched and white baby's breath filler in photo 3.

My inspiration for this flower is a drawing from a Nordic coloring book by Dover.

Hold the ends side by side (right) and mark placement lines on the other end. I had 2.5" of space at each end so I worked small flowers, berries and vines to stop 1" from ends for trimming.

I went back to the center and filled in some of the space with lazy daisy stitches, vines, and French knots.

The whole piece took me about 50 hours and I enjoyed every minute of it. Any project I can work on while I'm out and about or watching TV with the fam, I'm a big fan of!

When you take the fear out of working in this way, and cherish the time you have taken for yourself, I guarantee bliss. Common fears you may face are: Will I be judged? Will I like it after all the effort? Will I do it wrong? Am I creative enough? No. Yes. No. Yes. There you go. When you really examine these fears, they aren't really real. They stem from years of left-brain training and interacting with grouchy people. Tell it and them to be quiet! You're creating.

Step 3: Quilting.

With a hot steamy iron, press this section flat on the front and back. Mine measured 5.5"x32." I wanted this section to have a white border on either side to lighten it up and make it easier to add to the quilt. On the non-joining long side, I sewed a 1" white strip of fabric with a ¼" seam.

Cut a piece of batting and backing 7"x34" and make a sandwich. Work a basting line on 1/8" from the edge of the long sides which is okay as you will be joining with a white sashing. Use black thread to stipple quilt on just the black background around all the stitching you've done. You can do this in one thread as you meander in and around the embroidery shapes. This puffs up the motifs and adds even more texture. Almost like trapunto. I didn't do any quilting on the white strip.

Step 4: Trimming and Join with Sashing

Trim the short ends up so it matches the size of the main piece edge you're adding it onto (29.5" in our case). Trim the long side with the white strip (opposite of join). To do this, line up your acrylic ruler so that the ¾" line is placed on the seam between the black and white and trim.

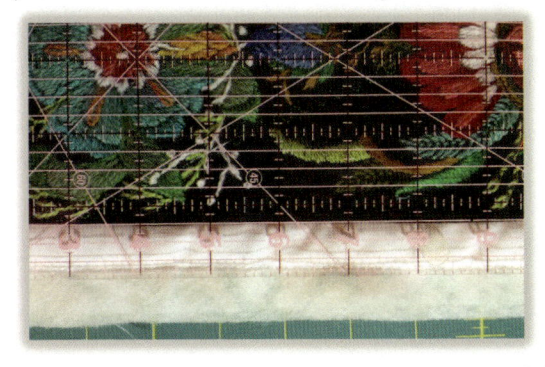

Cut a 1.5" of white and a 1" strip of backing fabric by 29.5." Follow the instructions on pages 39 and 40 for joining a section with sashing. The piece now measures 37.75"x29.5.

Here is my main piece so far. I find myself so curious as to what you and others have come up with. I would love for you to send me pictures of your progress (and permission to share them on my Facebook page if you'd like) and also any comments, ideas or questions that may have come up as you work through this book. I can learn as much from you as you can from me. If you have an easier way of doing things that others can benefit from, I welcome the opportunity to share your ideas with other quilters interested in pursuing this method of quilting as *inspired*. The more we share with each other, the better off our amazing quilting community will be.

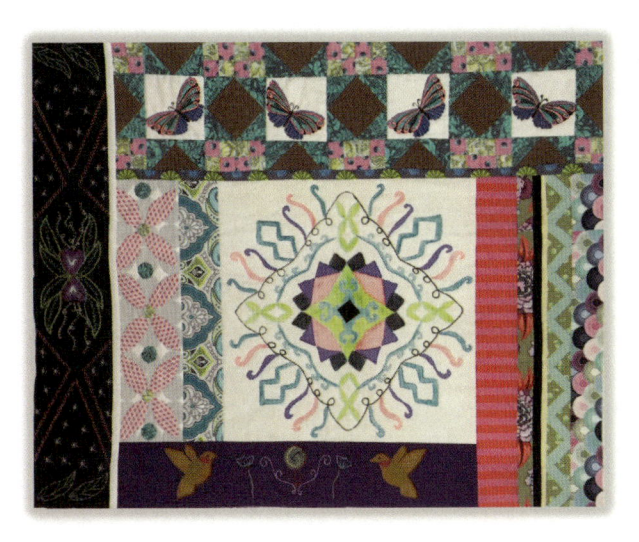

My wonderful mother, Cathy, a new quilter who veers more to the comforts of precise directions and traditional quilting, has generously donated her time and bravery to work through the book. It is helpful for me to watch her progress as she doesn't consider herself to be artistic at all. I completely disagree, but she stands firm. Rather than follow the Nordic theme, she drew out her own design for Section 1 and went from there. It came out festive and tropical which makes sense as she lived in Hawaii for over 10 years and loves going to Cajun music festivals. Her own inspirations are coming through while making the quilt. This is her work so far. I am crazy proud of my mom.

SECTION 7:
GLUE-BASTED, HAND PIECED HEXIES.

I love a hexie. So fun and versatile. I used to hand baste around hexies for English paper piecing, but I've updated my method to the skinny glue stick. Glue is the best thing that ever happened to the quilting industry. It's basically a replacement for pins and thread basting in many situations. Here, rather than hand stitching the pieces around paper template as we did in Section 2, we'll glue down the seam allowances in a fraction of the time it takes to hand stitch. I'm all about time savers as long as the work remains good. Plus this method is more accurate. And much faster. Win/win!

Materials:

Fabrics for Hexies: 4 fat quarters each of reds, oranges and 1 fat quarter each of stripes and florals. If you find this section has too much red and orange, of course you can use some greens and aqua blues to balance it out.
Fabric for Border: 1.5"x38" of floral fabric
Background Fabric 14"x40": where I have aqua
Backing and Batting 14"x40".
Templates: Copy paper and the provided templates.
Fabric Glue Stick by Apliquick or Sewline.
Threads: Aurafil for piecing, Mettler Red for Quilting.

Step 1: Copy the Template.

Trace the template on the next page with a straight edge and Sharpie. Label each piece. The center being 1, the surrounding trapezoids all 2, the triangles 3 and the edge triangles 4. This is more for orientation of the pieces rather than knowing which piece goes where, which is pretty obvious. Make all the numbers face the center. Do this before you make copies. You'll need about 4 or 5 copies as each piece can be used 3 or 4 times. Cut each hexie part out directly on the line. I made 13 hexies; 6 across the bottom and 7 on the top.

Step 2: Fabric Choices.

Assign each shape to a fabric. I decided that I wanted to keep it all warm tones so all of my number 1s were fussy cut into a flower; all my 2 shapes I fussy cut a striped fabric; all 3s were with oranges; and all 4 pieces were assigned to red fabrics. Prints and nearly solids are fine. And of course, if you want more or different colors in this section, try different combinations and/or values.

Step 3: Glue Baste

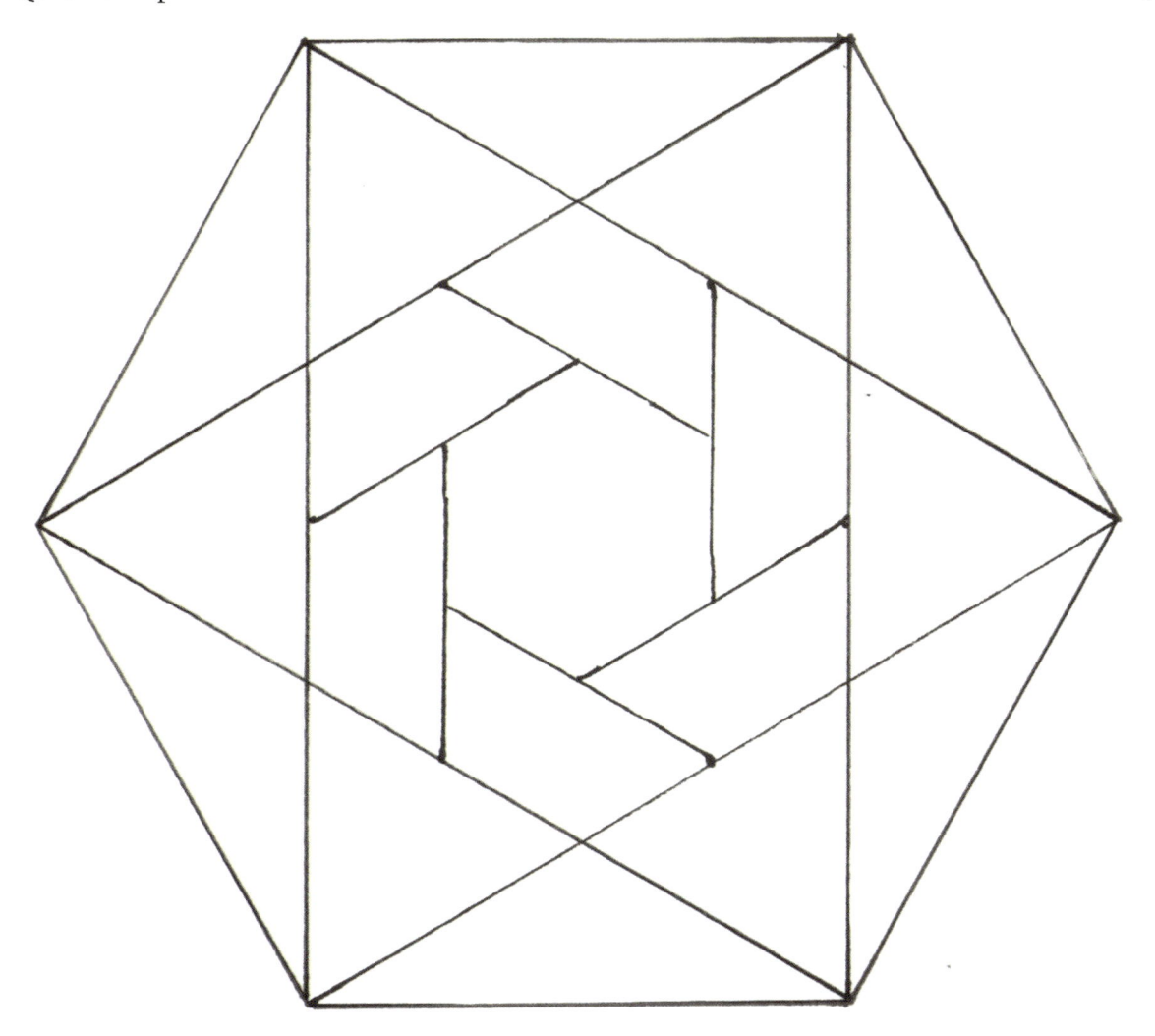

Pop a dab of glue on the back side of piece 1 and center it on the WS of a floral fabric. Cut around the piece with an approximate 1/3" seam. Gently swipe your glue stick along one side of the paper and fold the fabric down on top. A little light line of glue is good.

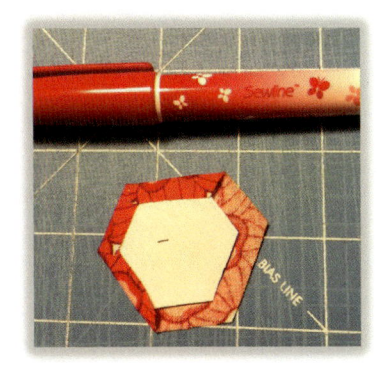

Work each shape in a clockwise direction, tucking the corners under on each side as you work. When you're done, you'll have a perfect hexie with crisp clean edges.

It is truly a revelation to glue these pieces to paper rather than hand baste. Faster, more accurate and a bit more fun. I can't see any reason to go back to hand basting. Give it a try! Honestly, I didn't believe the glue would come off so easily from the paper. But it did!

Group 2

For group 2, find a striped fabric and on the WS glue all 6 pieces on the same line so they all look alike. You could also find two different stripe patterns and alternate them around the center mini hexie as I did in a few instances.

Repeat the gluing process moving clockwise around each shape for all the edges. On the remaining pieces, you will get dog ears that stick out on two of the corners – don't cut them off. They'll end up on the WS like a true seam allowance.

When all your pieces are glued on, lay them out to keep them in order.

Sections 3 and 4 are pretty straight forward. Do all the 3 sections first.

When stitching the section 4s, you'll match up the first edge and start at the outside corner working down to the point, then open it up and refold the left edge down to the next section 3 triangle. You'll be working counterclockwise in between the 3s. However, lefties may be working clockwise.

Step 5: Hand Stitching.

Start by holding up a number 2 piece to a side of the mini center hexie RS together. As you can see, the left half the hexie hangs out over the edge to accommodate the next piece 2. With RS together, whipstitch the pieces every 1/16" taking only two threads of each piece per time. This is a tiny stitch done with a single strand of thread.

Don't cut the thread at the end. See above. You'll keep going with the same thread counterclockwise all the way around. Line up the third piece and fold it RS together with the first section 2 piece and continue stitching down the line so that you'll be attaching the short end of the new piece to the rest of the long end of the first piece 2.

When you reach the end, hide the thread under the seam and come out of the intersection where the 3 points meet at the corner of a hexie. Unfold and refold the new piece so you can sew the long side of that new piece to the next edge of the hexie. Continue around until all group 2 pieces are attached.

Step 6: Removing Paper and Pressing.

When your hexie is complete, gently remove the section 1-3 papers. Just run a fingernail under the seam and it will pop right off. Keep these aside and they can be reused a couple more times.

With the unit 4 papers still in, give it a good squirt and press to set the creases on the outside. When ironing the WS, I try to press the seams down as they want to naturally go. Now you can gently remove the unit 4 papers and keep them with its set. Repress hexie.

Time to start another hexie! This is such a great take along or sofa sitting project.

Step 7: Stitching Them Together

You'll make 13 hexies and stitch them together with a whipstitch as you did with the inner components. Take a few extra stitches where the 3 points of the triangles all come together to reinforce the corners and so the points match as best as you can.

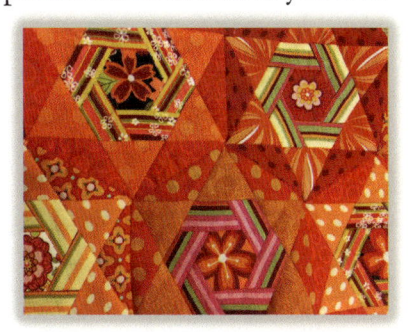

I actually stitched them together as I went along so that I had better direction when choosing fabrics for each next hexie. I wanted a random appearance, but didn't want any matching fabrics next to each other. It was just another help in narrowing it down.

You now have a giant applique piece with the outer edges turned under. You could fill in the shapes to make it square with diamonds and half hexies, but honestly, this hand-stitched section took a long time and I'm ready to finish it up and move on to the next section. I know I shouldn't say that, as I'm preaching my love for the slow stitch movement and working with intention here, but I do get to the point where I'm tired of looking at the same piece for a long stretch. Just keepin' it real.

Step 8: Make a Background.

Instead of more piecing, you're going to lay this unit on a background piece of fabric, machine applique it on, cut out the back of the fabric and quilt it as a unit.

Break out your 14"x40" background piece.

Pin the unit to the background fabric at the points and the angles, tucking in the dog ears and pinning under. I pinned one end down and stitched it, smoothed it out, pinned the other half and finished stitching just in case it got wonky. Of course, you can always use a bit of glue to help keep those dog ears in check.

Step 9: Machine Applique:

Use the applique stitch on your machine to stitch it down. Remove the pins as you go and use the aid of tweezers or a stylus to tuck any of the dogears that pop out. Lift pressure foot every few inches to smooth out the fabrics.

Turn unit over and cut out the center of the stitched section out ¼" away from the stitch line to save fabric and reduce bulk.

Step 10: Trim and Add a Border.

Line up your ruler so the ¼" marking lines up with the points of one long side of the hexie and trim.

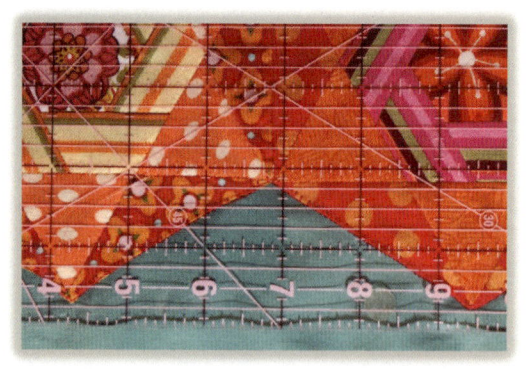

Cut a 1.5" border strip out of a floral fabric and stitch it to the side you just trimmed. If you sew with the hexie piece side up, you can run your needle along the points to make sure you don't cut the points off:

This floral sashing strip is the joining side.

On the other long side, line the ruler so that the ¼" mark matches the points and trim. Cut the short ends so the piece measures ½" longer on each side than the MP side you're adding on to allow for quilting shrinkage.

Make the quilt sandwich and ditch the seam line of the border sashing and ditch all the way around the entire outer border of the hexies. I did not ditch the inner seams of the hexies. Baste the other non-joining long edge and short edges 1/8" from the raw edges.

Step 11: The Quilting.

I went to the outline drawing of the hexie so as not to be influenced by color or pattern and drew out a couple of options of quilting patterns. I liked the third option a lot so I went with that. With red thread, I started in the center of the hexie to do the petals, then with the same thread, worked on the section 2 petals (piggyback on one short line of the mini hexie to get to an outer point first). I then worked my way out to quilt the section 3s by piggybacking on a seam to get to the mid section of a 3 triangle. *I stitched up to the top middle of a section 4 piece, then back down to the middle of the next 3 triangle. Work the double tiered upside down triangles in section 3, and continue around the hexie and repeat from *. I changed the double radiating lines that work into section 4 into a single line or the flow wouldn't be right. At the end of the hexie, I stopped and tied off and then started a new thread for the next hexie. You can find this demo on my YouTube channel.

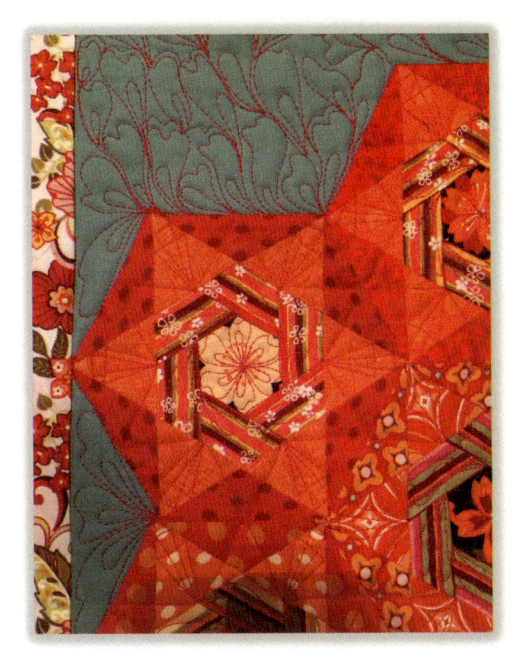

On the aqua triangle spaces between the hexies, I repeated the wonky petal motifs and stitched 3 petals in each space. On the shorter ends, I stitched overlapping petals to fill the space. I did no quilting on the floral border.

These are little blue grippers that I can't quilt without. You can also use quilting gloves. Either is helpful to prevent your hands from slipping off the fabric. Up until now, we haven't needed them, but the pieces are getting bigger and we need more grip because of the weight.

Press and trim the quilted section to the size of the MP, which is 37.75" long (center the hexie strip within) and 11.75" wide (not including the excess bat and back). Trim the floral border side so that you end up with the required ¼" extra bat and back protruding from the raw edge. Add this piece to the main piece as instructed in detail on page 25. The piece now measures approx. 40.75"x37.75."

SECTION 8:
NORDIC STAR BLOCKS

This is a 9" **un**finished block which is not a traditional size. This is because I drafted an easy to draw unfinished 8.5" block to then add a ½" white sashing with a tiny black square in the middle for interest. Each half square triangle in the block will measure 2.5" unfinished.

Materials:

Fabrics: ½ yard white; 1 fat quarter each of black, turquoise, green and a lighter print turquoise and print green.
Batting/Backing Fabric 45"x11": Use extra piece of backing from a previous section and piece to get 45."
Threads: I used Mettler Silk Finish in a light aqua for quilting and Aurafil grey for piecing.

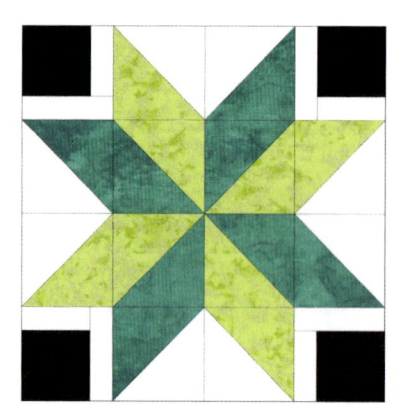

You could cut each shape and then sew them together, but the diagonal seams are on the bias and are a bit harder to manage, so a better way to make these squares are to sew first and cut after. Known better as half square triangles. To do this you'll cut a square for each color that is 7/8" bigger than the FINISHED square measurement. In this case, 2 7/8" squares. I like wiggle room, so we're rounding the measurement up to 3."

To cut squares, I'll cut 3" strips of each color first, then simply cut the appropriate size square (3" here). For the sashing white pieces, cut 1" strips and then cut the sizes needed.

Step 1: Cutting Details.

Cutting instructions are for one block. You are making 5 total so just multiply the amounts of each piece by 5. Again, accuracy is key. I actually like to put my 12" Quilter's Cut and Press on my lap and really focus on the small cuts with smaller rulers and rotaries. This also has an ironing surface on the other side, so you can press anything that has a crease or wrinkle before you cut out the shapes.

> Black: Four 2" squares and one 1" square
> White: Four EACH of 3" squares; 1x2" pieces; 1x2.5" pieces; 1x4.5" pieces;
> Turquoise: Two 3" squares;
> Light Turquoise print: Two 3" squares
> Green: Two 3" squares
> Light Green print: Two 3" squares

The drawing above is the basic block without the sashing showing just two colors for the turquoise and green. As you can see from my quilt photo, I used a lighter print green and lighter print turquoise for each point of the star. You can, of course, just use two colors. Or 8 for that matter.

Step 2: Sew Half Square Triangles.

Match up all the square fabrics you've cut with their coordinating color RS together. Each square pair will make two half square triangle units. Here you'll match 2 white squares each with a lighter green print and 2 white squares each with a lighter turquoise print. Then match 2 green squares with 2 turquoise squares. This will give you 4 half square triangles of each color combo unit. Take it slow. See below.

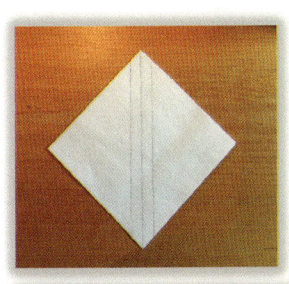

With a Frixion pen and a ruler, draw a line down the diagonal center of the lighter square and then two lines ¼"on either side. The center line is the cutting line and the others are sewing lines.

Do this for each of the 6 sets for each block. As always, I did one full block to make sure I liked it and then I chain pieced the other four blocks.

Step 3: Serious Chain Piecing.

Chain piece one side of all four blocks at once then turn it around and chain piece the other side. Then cut them apart.

You now have a big pile of chain piecey goodness. Cut the two threads in between each one and then cut them apart down the center line. Open them up and press each seam to the darker color.

Step 4: Square Up the HSTs.

These need to measure 2.5" unfinished so now's the time to square them up. Of course you can use your mat and normal acrylic ruler to do this. Just make sure the diagonal line runs to each corner before you cut. I am a huge fan of the Creative Grid square rulers that have the .5" built right in. These are invaluable for squaring stuff up. They're a bit pricy so every time I go to the quilt shop I treat myself to a new size. Here is my 2.5" ruler that I use all the time. Note the diagonal line. Cut off all ears. Set these aside in 4 individual block piles for now.

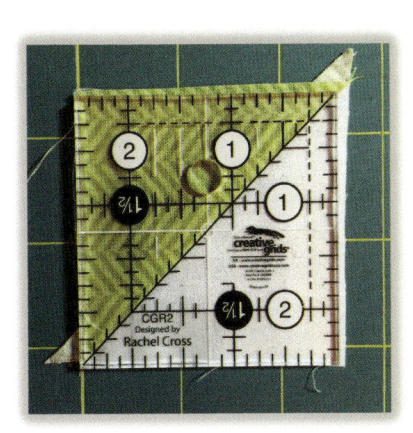

Step 5: Corner Squares

Take your larger black squares and the shorter white strips. Chain piece a 2" white strip along one side of each black square. Cut apart and then finger press open and with the white strip on top, place a 2.5" strip on the right side of the unit and chain piece all the units. Cut apart. Press all seams to the white fabric. Trim to 2.5"

Step 6: Putting it Together.

Lay the units out in quads as follows:

Chain piece the squares together, keeping the units in a row (i.e., sew the upper left black and white piece to its right white/aqua neighbor, then sew the white/green square below it to its right green/blue square). Then continue in this manner for each quad unit. When they are all chain pieced, cut them apart in pairs so when you take them over to the ironing board, you can manage pressing the seams of the pairs in the opposite direction for easier piecing.

Now sew the pairs together into 4 patches. But stop there. Don't sew the 4 patches together because we want to put the sashing in between. Once sewn, put them back into piles like the photo above.

Take the left upper and lower quads and place a 4.5" long white strip along the right edge of each and chain piece all 8. Finger press open so seam is toward the white strip. On the other side of the strip attach the matching right quads. Press seams toward the white strip.

Sew a 1" black square between 2 short ends of remaining white strips for a total of 4 times. These pieced strips will be sewn in between the block halves to make a 9" block. Press seams toward the white strip. Sew 5 blocks together in a line making sure black squares line up with each other.

Step 7: The Quilting.

Use a transparency sheet to audition a few different designs or if you are an iPad user, import a photo of the block and draw some patterns. Here is what I ended up with:

Make your quilt sandwich and baste the long edge opposite the joining side. The only thing I ditched was the large white diamond that formed in between the stars. I normally would ditch the star, but since we're not joining with sashing, I couldn't outline the whole thing without going over the ½" space needed to join on the one side. Tape down the joining side and ditch the diamonds now.

Each block gets it's own thread. I started at a corner of the center black square and worked a feather that reached up into the black corner box. Although the drawing doesn't show, I echo quilted around the feather. I then proceeded to the next side (white strip) and worked some leaf shapes and a little feather coming from the center. Note that the horizontal leaf/feather spokes are longer than the vertical. We are not joining with a sashing and again, we don't want to go beyond the tape.

After each block was done, I went into the white diamonds and quilted a little spoke of leaf shapes and feather on the adjacent sides so that the tips of the four feathers came close together in the center of the diamond. For me that is still a big white space. Some strategically placed applique may have to go there. But I can decide that later.

This section now measures approx. 41.5"x8.75" and is an inch too long for the side of the MP. Since this is supposed to look like a quilt that was put together from many different textiles, I'm okay to cut off that inch. The star effect is still there. If you just can't do it, turn to page 63 for an alternative fix. If you're trimming to fit, join it to the MP as instructed on page 25. The quilt now measures 46"x40.5.

SECTION 9:
BORDER STRIPS AND WHITE WORK

As I look at the piece so far, I'm happy with the way it's coming together. With the previous Nordic Star section, however, there is a lot of white negative space and the quilt sections are getting bigger. For Section 9, I want to bring back a few narrow strips to coordinate with the Fair Isle section and a bit of embroidery (not nearly as much as before) to be harmonious with Section 6.

Materials:

Fabrics: 4"x47" blue strip for the white work; two 1"x47" bright solid (yellow) strips; two 2"x47" small print (tree stems); and one - 3.5"x47" inspiration fabric. Obviously, you can use whatever colors you want, but I'll be referring to my colors for ease of placement instructions. You'll have to piece all of these.
Interfacing 4.5"x47": For the structure to stitch white work. I used Pellon SF101.
Backing and Batting: 48"x12" Piece the back with leftover of previous cut; piece batting with a 2"x12" strip of interfacing.
White work thread: Size 10 mercerized crochet cotton. I used DMC Cebelia.
Threads: I used White Mettler for the quilting.
Sewline Chalk or Frixion Pen for Marking.

Which Way is Up?
It's time to start thinking about the orientation of the quilt and whether it will be square or rectangle. This will be a queen size quilt (60"x80") which means I need to design more specifically the sizes of the last 4 sections 10-13 as well as the techniques I want to play with. I'll talk more on this at end of this Section as that is the point where we have gone twice around the center block.

Step 1: Assemble the Background.
Sew the long sides of the strips together. Start with the blue center and add a yellow strip to each side, then the small print on either side of that. The inspiration fabric gets attached to just one side and this will be the side we'll join to the MP. Press all seams to the outside of the strip. Fuse your strip of interfacing to the WS so that it covers the entire center section and the ½" bright borders. This will stabilize the piece enough. The piece is 11" tall.

I used a few decorative machine stitches. On the yellow borders, I stitched a line of tulips, did some scroll work on the sides and a created a fun flowery center line which helps in keeping the line of embroidery right down the middle.

This is the stitching of one half of the motif. See the simple drawing of the full motif above. The smaller elements to the right of the large flower are repeated in a mirror image on the left side of it. I stitched three motifs total and then worked a few of the small flowers and leaves at the ends.

Get your hoop, sharp needle and white thread. This stitching will go faster than Section 6. There's nothing new here that you haven't seen in the embroidery stitches from Section 3. Work back stitch for the flowers and leaves; and stem stitches for the vines. Work some stab stitches at each ends of the leaves for detail and make lazy daisy details inside the big petals. Below you can see I satin stitched the edges of the flowers and whip stitched around the lines of the tulips. When working satin and whipstitch, make sure you surround the outline. And no embroidery is complete without a few French knots.

When the embroidery is finished, press it out with a hot steamy iron and a pressing cloth. Make your quilt sandwich and baste the long edge opposite the joining side and tape the edge that you'll be attaching to the MP since you're not joining with a sashing.

The quilting on this goes fast. There is no marking and mostly ditching and straight-line quilting. Hopefully, that makes up for all the handwork you did on this section. It did for me.

Step 3: The Quilting.

Start by ditching the seam between the inspiration fabric and the small print and then 2 seams between the bright yellow and the print. Alternate the ends you start with. Rather than ditching between yellow and blue, I worked a line of straight stitching 1/8" from the edge (left). I chose an "S" curving line from my decorative stitches and ran two lines of quilting on the inspiration fabric. All this was done with white thread before attaching the free motion foot.

The only free motion quilting I did for this section was two rows of echo stitching around the outside of the hand work (in blue thread) and on the green stems, I quilted down the line and did an occasional (every fourth leaf) outline of the little leaves every other side of the stem. Once you're done with the quilting, press, trim with the excess bat/back (piece measures 46"x10.5" not including extra bat and back), and join to the MP as we did on page 25.

You've gone twice around. The two quilts below are the same photo but turned different ways so you can see how different the quilt looks simply by rotating it. If we were keeping the quilt square, it wouldn't matter so much, but in this case we want a rectangle to fit atop a queen size bed so it is important to know which way is up. We also need to measure the quilt so we can anticipate the size and orientation of the last 4.

The photo on the left is more visually pleasing. The flower motifs of Section 5 are right side up and I do like the blue trim going across the top. In addition, the visual weight of the red hexie section would be a bit unsettling to have on the sides or at the top (see right), so it feels natural to turn it so that section is at the bottom. My birds are upside down, but I have to look at something right side up while snuggling under the quilt, right?

At this point, the quilt measures 46"x50.5." The next section will run down the left side (see photo on the left above). I want to do a traditional quilt block that incorporates all the colors I've used so far in the quilt. What better than log cabin blocks in this quilt building? You can use lots of leftover fabrics and they go quickly. Read on!

Section 10:
The Log Cabin Inside the Log Cabin

Make seven 8" blocks (unfinished). Going in, you know that this section might be a bit big for the MP edge to attach it to. When they're all sewn together, it will measure around 53." It's hard to know how much shrinkage will occur during quilting. The next section will be called Section 9.1: Addendum. Fixing Size Issues. You can skip to that now, or do Section 10 first, which is obviously what I did. Making and quilting Section 10 and then going back to lengthen Section 9 will at least give you an idea of how much you'll need to add, if any at all. Your quilt may be a bit bigger or smaller than mine at this point.

Materials:

Fabrics: Here is where you can likely dip into leftovers. See the cutting list under Step 1 below.
Batting and Backing Fabrics 55"x10." Piece the backing and perhaps the batting with interfacing.
Copy paper: You'll learn how to make your own quilting template guide in this section.
Clear thread: or any color you'd like. Clear can be tricky and will take some practice and tension manipulation.
Buttons: 7 Black basic buttons to adorn the center of each log cabin.

Step 1: Log Cabin Fabrics.

Log cabin blocks are most effective when the two pairs of adjacent sides are of different kinds of fabrics such as light and dark; print and solid; or in our case, cool and warm colors. See below. If you squint, you'll see the diagonal line that separates our two types of fabrics.

From top to bottom is the order I added each square *clockwise* around the center square this time. You can go either way around, just be consistent.

Step 2: Cut Strips of Fabric.

Refer to the photo on the left as you cut the strips. The cutting instructions are for one block, but you'll lay out and string piece all 8 blocks at once. To begin, cut one set and line up the colors in the block formation to make sure you love it.

Black square (center):	2" square
White mini dot:	1.5"x2"
White and black print:	1.5"x3"
Yellow and pink stripe:	1.5"x3"
Pink floral print:	1.5"x4"
Light green print:	1.5"x4"
Light aqua print:	1.5"x5"
Red floral:	1.5"x5"
Red and orange dot:	1.5"x6"
Green print:	1.5"x6"
Turquoise:	1.5"x7"
Red and orange print:	1.5"x7"
Dark red dot:	1.5"x8"

To streamline the process, cut 1.5" strips of each fabric and then cut lengths from the strips. Line them up for easy string piecing.

Step 3: Make the Blocks

The sewing goes smoothly if you chain piece the blocks in an assembly line. In other words, sew all the first strips to the center squares in one big chain, cut apart, finger press open so that the seam goes towards the strip. Place those in a pile with the new strips toward the top, and then sew the second strip to the right edge of the block. Repeat this process until all the strips are attached and the block measures 8" unfinished. Press flat on both sides, making sure all the seams are facing towards the outside of the block. Trim the blocks so they measure the 8" and the edges are straight.

Step 4: Orient the Blocks and Join

The great thing about the log cabin block, other than being so simple to construct, is that the entire look of a quilt can change based solely on the way you turn the blocks and sew them together. Experiment with lining up your blocks in different ways, take a few shots with your phone or camera and compare them to see which you prefer.

Once you've decided on the orientation, join them together and trim so that you have a long strip that will run down the left side of the quilt.

Step 5: Make A Quilting Template:

Use your original drawing from the center section to copy a motif to quilt. I used a portion of the central design. Here is a square of regular copy paper placed over the freezer paper to trace ¼ of the design. Place this on your light box and trace the lines you'd like to quilt. You can select which lines to use and even add some new ones to make the quilting of the adjusted motif go smoother. You're simply taking some lines from your initial inspiration.

Storage Workstation

I'd like to take this opportunity to share with you my little workstation storage invention unit. In the past, I have found myself struggling with how to keep all my applique, tracing implements, and small cutting tools in one place so I can just plop down and work without all that hunting and gathering.

I went over to the Container Store and purchased this heavy cardboard 2-drawer storage box and miniature bulletin board. The board came with adhesive strips, so I attached it to the top of the box. Now when I need to draw applique pieces onto fabric or cut stencils or fabric with a craft blade, I can simply pin the pieces to the board and not have to hold them with my hands or tape anything down, which can be so cumbersome. Plus. Storage! This works great on a low coffee table or, if you're like me, sitting crisscross applesauce on the floor or couch while watching TV. In this case, you'll actually be cutting out the main shape with scissors instead of using a blade, but if you need to cut a stencil for any of your designs in the future, use vellum, newsprint or butcher paper and an X-acto knife. It works great and you can easily see through all those papers to trace. Copy paper is bonded and harder to cut with a blade.

Step 6: The Quilting.

Since we're not joining with a sashing, plan out the ditching and quilting accordingly. Choose which side you like better for the join. In my quilt, I liked the red border on the outside as it gives the look of a frame for the left side. Baste your non-joining side with a 1/8" seam, tape down over that ½" of the joining side, then ditch the seams separating the blocks starting at the basted edge and stopping ½" away from the joining edge and knotting just to be safe. The quilting of a log cabin can be very easy. Use your walking foot to run along all the seams. It is beautiful in its simplicity and an effective way to make the strips of the log cabin blocks stand out.

If you want to try something more intricate, see what I did. If you're going to use monofilament thread, practice with this first. Go slow. Play with tension. In the bobbin, use the same thread or something even thinner. Since I'm just trying to get placement of main lines and not doing an intricate pattern, it's sufficient to cut out a shape that will help with that. The heart is hanging on by a paper thread. I try to do the least amount of marking as humanly possible. Lazy, you see.

Left, I traced around the entire design, in the heart spaces and then drew an extra line from the V of the heart up to the scroll.

At right, my design is traced all the way around. BTW, my template is pink because I tried a Frixion highlighter. Which is not so great on red. Duh.

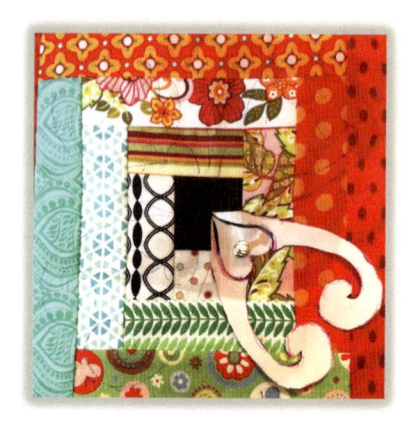

Each block gets its own thread. With clear, I started at the V of a heart, worked towards the right and quilted all the other hearts around and completed the first heart where I started. I then echoed the heart around in the same direction. For the outer scrolls, I quilted up that extra drawn line to the scroll, back down the middle line to the V of the heart, piggybacking up the extra line, worked my way around the outer part of the scroll, which ended me at a point between scrolls. I worked the next outer scroll to the right and quilted the same lines but in reverse, which piggybacked the extra drawn line and ended me up in the V of the heart. YouTube. When in doubt of how you're going to quilt something, outline it first with pencil and paper to practice.

On another note, normally with black or dark fabrics, I'll use the dark smoke clear thread. It's hard to tell from the photo, but the clear thread that came together in the center square makes a weird looking knot. This is a great time for some strategically-placed black buttons in the center of the blocks, which look great. Another design opportunity.

We'll be joining this to the quilt as per the instructions on page 25, but as you may have already read, this new section is too long for the MP. I knew going in just by doing simple math 8" blocks multiplied by 7 = 56" minus 3" in joining gives a strip measurement of 53." The small amount of quilting I did didn't shrink the section too much and it now measures 7.75"x52.5." The side of my quilt measures 50.5" Without much quilting on this section, I was aware there might have to be a fix. Working with improvisation can have its challenges, but there is always a way out.

SECTION 9-1: ADDENDUM.
FIXING SIZE ISSUES.

This is what it looks like after it's been quilted. Chopping off any part of the log cabin section is not an option this time, as I really like the effect of the strip. So I'll need to add an additional piece onto the top of the MP. This is great because I've been wanting to incorporate some of the lace trims that have been sadly lying around my studio collecting dust. There was, and maybe still is, some lacemaking happening in that region so it's a great way to pay homage to those incredible craftspeople. I can tat, knit and crochet lace all day, but when it comes to actual lacemaking with bobbins and pins, I'm completely clueless. But I am always intrigued with crafts I don't know how to do, so I'm sure I'll have to pick up that skillset at some point. Because I need one more hobby.

To some, this all may seem a bit too … devil may care, especially to those who are accustomed to making tops with very precise instructions and measurements. If this is your thinking, I respect and understand how this might seem like we're just doing a bunch of disorganized rectifying. And you'd be right. But that's what design is. **Designing is solving problems**. It may take a bit of mind opening and letting go of control, perfection or precision to quilt in this way. But if you can learn to adapt to quilting as you're inspired, I cannot stress enough how liberating it is to cross the bridges as you come to them and know that you have the cleverness to get resourceful, get creative and come up with a beautiful solution. You, the artist is born. Remember, there are no mistakes, just happy accidents. I forever channel Bob Ross. Genius.

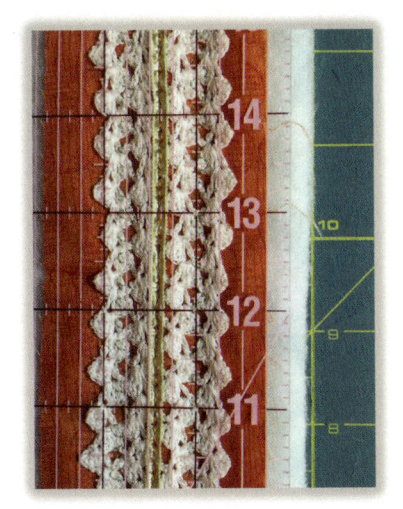

Cut an orange strip of fabric 2.5"x46"
Cut backing and batting 3"x48."
Make a quilt sandwich with the three layers.
Find a trim that measures 1.75"x46" and a 46" length of ribbon yarn that measures and pin it to the top layer so that you have ¼" space on one side and ½" on the other. The ¼" is the joining side.

Center the ribbon yarn on the trim and quilt a long straight line down the length of the ribbon. Quilt two more straight lines ¼" away on either side of the center line to secure the trim. On the joining side, line your ruler up so that the ¼" line runs along the top layer and trim leaving that excess ¼" of batting and backing required for joining. Trim the other long edge. Attach the new strip to the top of the quilt as instructed on page 25. Now your MP should measure the 52.5" for the log cabin strip to be attached. Follow the same method to join Section 10 as on page 25. All is well and it only cost just a bit of extra hand stitching. With trimming and squaring up, the piece now measures 52.25"x53.25."

SECTION 11:
A LITTLE CABIN IN THE WOODS

As I study Nordic folk art history, my mind keeps wandering to the people cozied up in their homes in their villages, embroidering by the hearth when the hard work of the day was done. So why not add at the bottom of the quilt some trees and a cabin with yellow candlelit windows to let us know someone is home. I imagine someone stitching by the fire. That is the beauty in designing this way. At the beginning of this project, the thought of doing this piece never entered my mind. It's like the quilt is telling its own story and I'm the vessel in which to create it.

Materials:

Fabrics: Lots of leftover scraps and pieces can be used. Here is what I chose:
  Trees: ½ yard blue for sky; fat quarter scraps of 4 different greens; 2 different browns or olives
  House: same blue for sky; 2 different roof colors; light print for house; darker strip for corner; yellow flannel scraps for windows;
  Borders: Black strip 57"x2.5"; Floral Strip for bottom 57"x4" (exact length will be same as tree/cabin strip.)
Backing and Batting 18"x60": And an additional 1"x54" back strip for joining with sashing
Sashing: 1.5"x54" Black and white print strip
Thread and Floss: I used several different threads to quilt and a thin white cotton size 10 to embroider stars

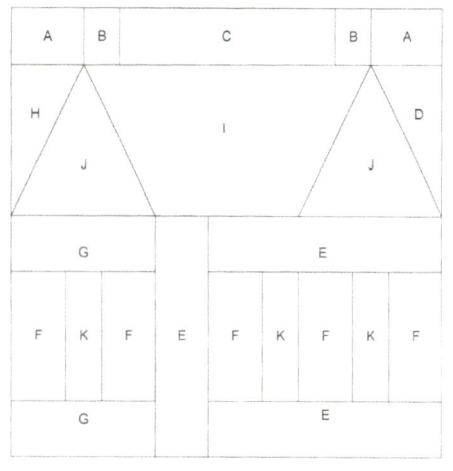

Step 1: Rotary Cut Rectangle Patches:
A: Sky blue. Rotary cut two patches 2.25"x1.75"
B: Red print. Rotary cut two patches 1.25"x1.75"
C: Sky blue. Rotary cut one patch 5.5"x1.75"
E: Ochre/House. Rotary cut one ochre and two house patches 1.75"x6"
F: House Print. Rotary cut five patches 1.75"x3.5"
G: House Print. Rotary cut two patches 3.75"x1.75"
K: Yellow wool. Rotary cut three patches 1.25"x3.5"

Step 2: Template Cut Angled Patches:
D: Sky blue. Template cut one patch - instructions next page.
H: Sky blue. Template cut one patch using the reverse side of D.
I: Roof stripe. Template cut one patch.
J: Roof dot. Template cut two patches.

Of course, use any colors you want, I will refer to mine for ease of instruction and placement.

A Word on Designing a Block

You can cut any size shape you want by drawing a square of the finished size you need and making lines to create shapes within that block. Cut out each shape on the line and when cutting fabric, add a ¼" seam allowance to the shape. I realize this may sound terrifying and I'm not going to suggest you do that here. It's just worth knowing that this is possible. Instead, I'm giving you the templates and rotary cutting instructions. I'm big on knowing how to do achieve a task with the most basic of tools. It gives us a true understanding of the nature of what we are trying to accomplish. Not only that, what if all the power goes out for days at a time and we have to work by candlelight? And it snows and snows until the doors are blocked and we can't leave the house? It could happen. If you ever feel unsure about how to achieve a task, ask yourself this: "What would Laura Ingalls Wilder do?" It is amazing how resourceful you can be when you put this perspective-building question into your mind. If she could do it back in the day, we can certainly do it now. And I fully admit. I'm an enormous fan of Little House on the Prairie. I own them all. Charles Ingalls was perfect. Ok, sorry. Tangent much?

Having said all of that, I do like to utilize the time-saving tools available to us now. Check out the computer program called EQ7 that is fantastic for playing with blocks and colors and designs. You can print both templates and rotary cutting instructions for any block. And plus you get to color.

Step 2a: Cut Templates.

Trace or copy the templates on the next page and cut them out on the line. Make a couple of copies of the cabin and color a few options. Make sure you have enough blue for the sky in the tree blocks if you want the blues from the house to match like I did. My rough estimation is between ¼ and ½ yard.

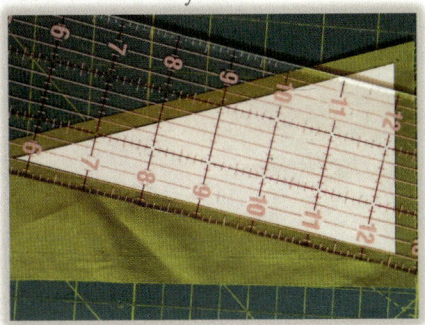

Place the template on the WS of the chosen fabric (above is from a tree block) and place a dot at each corner with a Frixion pen. It's helpful to place a small piece of tape so the template doesn't slide around. Place your ruler on the template so the ¼" mark lines up with the edge of the template and make a cut along the edge. Do this for all sides.

You can also draw a line around the template then pin and stitch along the line. I work in this way when doing curved piecing where you would also put in adjacent crossing registration marks for placement.

Step 3: The Cabin Components.

I used a combo platter of techniques to execute the blocks for this section. Through my piecing practice, I find I'm more accurate using templates with triangles and diamonds. They take a bit longer than rotary cutting from strips, but it's worth it as I get good results. With square and rectangle shapes, I can't be bothered with template making so I just rotary cut the size I need.

As you can see from the photos, only the roof strip has angle shapes, so I made templates for those and cut strips for the rest of the pieces. This may seem a bit unorthodox, but I find the quickest and most efficient way of completing a task. I have a lot of ideas running around in my head that need to be realized into art pieces so I don't focus on perfection and time-consuming rules. However, I always try to do my best work. There is a BIG difference between expecting perfection, and doing your best.

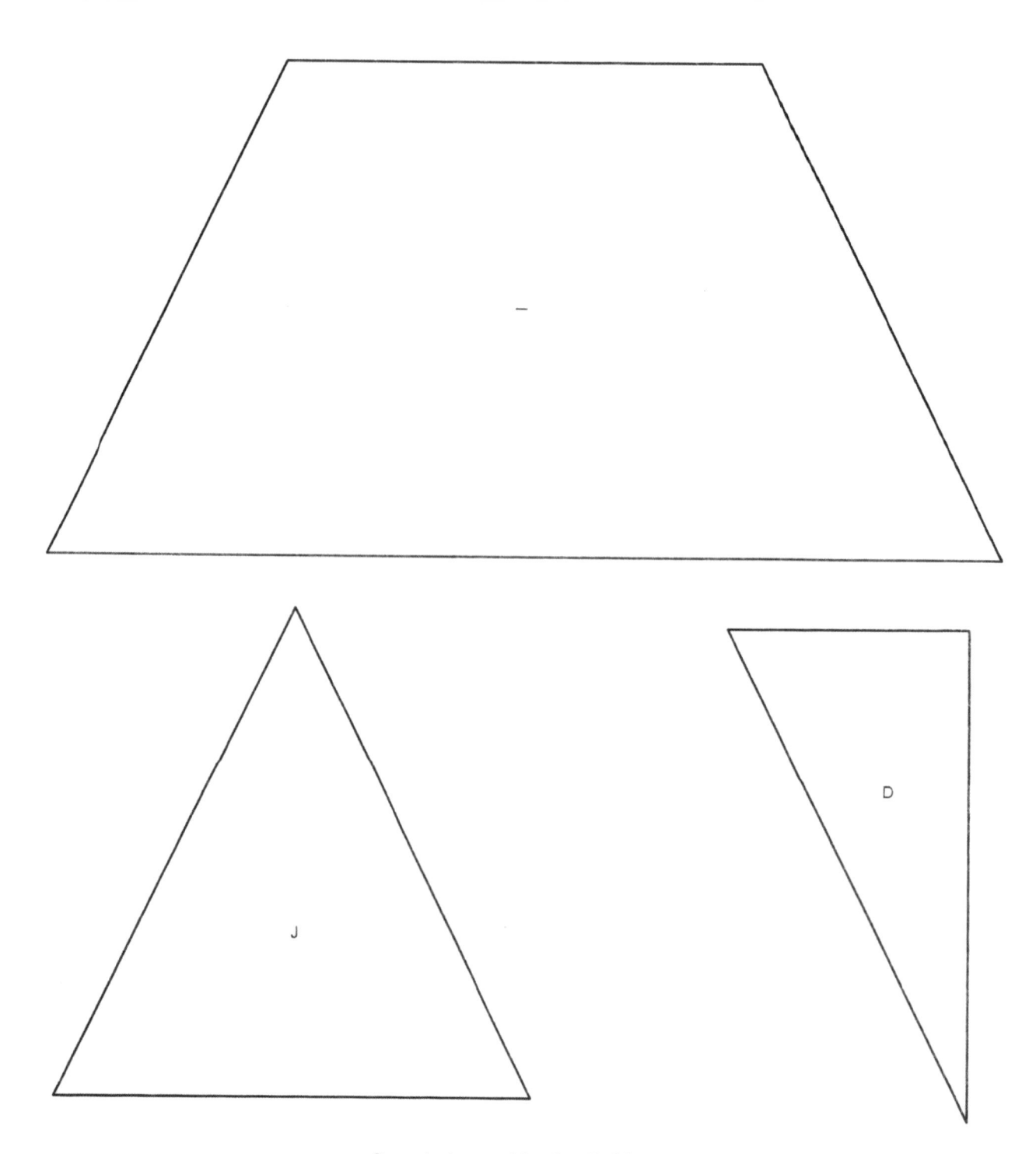

Step 4: Assemble the Cabin.

Notice how the Cabin block has three distinct horizontal pieced strip sections: the sky and chimney; the roof and side skies; and the rest of the house. That's how you're going to proceed. Using a ¼" seam allowance, piece together all of the units in their respective strips so you have something that looks like the photo on the next page.

When piecing the roof strip, place a pin in the dots you made on the WS of the fabrics to line up placement for the angles. See photo on tree assembly on page 69.

When piecing the house strip, put together the F and K pieces first, then sew the horizontal E and G patches on the tops and bottoms, then join them together with the vertical E ochre house patch.

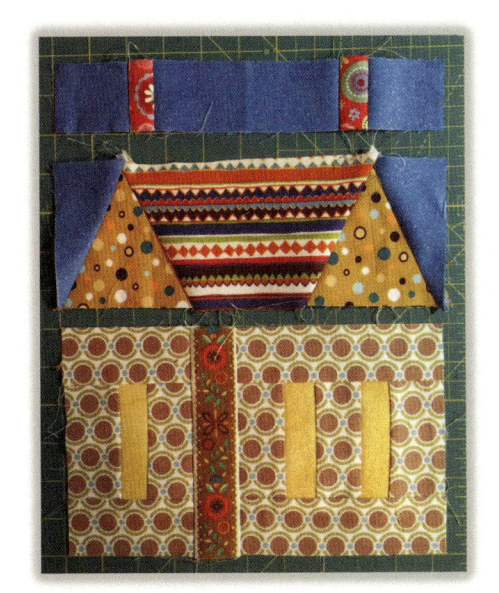

The top strip measures 10.5"x1.75"
The roof strip measures 10.5"x3.75"
The house strip measures 10.5"x6"

Square up and trim any rough edges of your strip sets and then line up the chimney patches with the roof and place pins. Line up the vertical cabin corner strip with the angled line of the rooftop and place a pin. Stitch the 3 rows together with a ¼" seam allowance.

Trim and square up the block to 10.5" square. Set aside.

Step 5: Rotary Cut Tree Patches:
A: Sky/ground. Cut 2 sky and 1 ground patch 3 7/8"x3"
B/C: Sky. Cut four strips 10"x2.25" for now.
D/I: Sky. Cut six strips 9"x2.25" for now.
E: Ground. Cut patch 3 7/8"x1 3/8"
F: Ground. Cut patch 3 7/8"x2 ¼"
G/H: Sky. Cut four strips 8"x2.25" for now.

Step 6: Template Tree Patches:
J: Tree. Template cut six trees.
K: Tree. Template cut four trees.
L: Tree. Template cut four trees.
NOTE: I used just 4 green fabrics for all

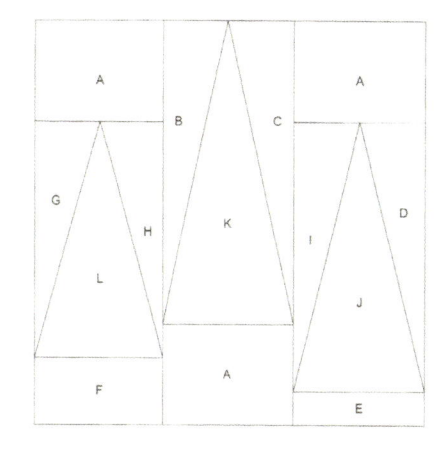

Shown above is the tree block containing 3 trees, which would measure 10.5" square. Since each tree unit is made separately, I treated each unit like its own skinny mini block and arranged them in different places rather than assembling them back into a whole 10.5" block.

Each of the tree templates gets its own set of surrounding sky triangles as you can see in the key block. (i.e., tree L goes with sky G/H).

Templates would be fine for this, but since the strip height is the same for all the trees, I decided to cut both the sky pieces at the same time as shown in the following photos. The great thing is that the cut will give you four pieces that you can use for two tree blocks.

You'll find the templates for the trees and rotary instructions for the sky and ground patches on the next page. I made 14 but only used 13 trees. I did a lot of quilting and mine shrunk so much that it was a 1/2" too small for the piece. I will show a fix for that, but just a heads up: if you don't want to have that happen, just add that 14th tree block and cut part of it off later. Easier than the fix, but I did want to show you how to remedy a piece that may end up too short for you in the future.

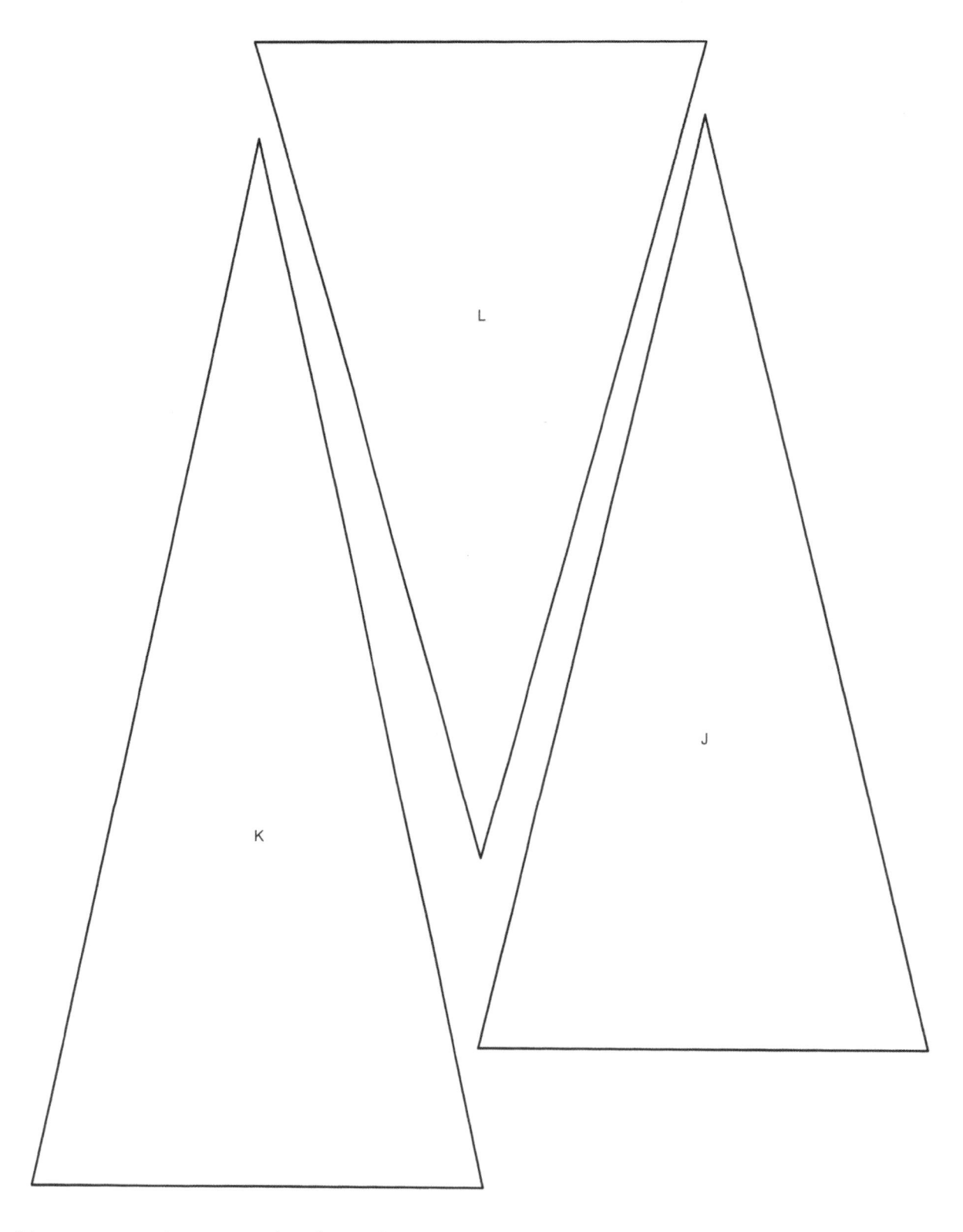

Trace or copy the true-to-size shapes from this page onto regular copy paper and cut the trees on the line. Like the roof patches shown previously, these do not include a ¼" seam allowance. You'll add that on the fabric like you did for the roof templates shown on the page 65. You won't need duplicates of the templates as these can be reused.

Cut all of the sky triangles by placing two of the same length sky strips (let's say the 10" strips B and C) on your cutting surface with RS together as shown at left. Hold your ruler on top of the pair diagonally so the cutting edge goes from one corner to its diagonal corner and make your cut. This will give you four pieces: two of each sky patch for two trees. Repeat for all the other strips and place them with their appropriate tree. In the 10" case, with tree K.

I went to make these patches one at a time, but one cut out of one piece of fabric RS up gives two identical pieces. Just flip the fabric over and you get the opposite piece. Cut them both at the same time and you'll get four! I always learn these things the hard way. But it gets ingrained deeper in the brain. Better for the long run.

Once you have your sky and ground patches cut out, place those with their corresponding skinny mini tree block and you're ready to sew. I didn't chain piece here, it felt more natural to get each individual tree done as I went, but you may feel differently and decide to chain. That's okay!

Step 7: Assemble the Trees

When sewing these deep angles, I like to place a pin in the dots of both pieces as we did for our roof strip. That's great until one of those pieces is rotary cut like our skies in this case. Make sure that a pin gets placed in the tree top dot and ¼" away from the top and side edges of the corresponding sky piece. See left. Sew the other sky piece the same way and trim those crazy long dog-ears. Make sure you have at least ¼" space at the top of your tree! Sew on the appropriate sky and ground pieces for each tree block and you'll have 14 mini trees ready to go.

Each tree should measure 3 7/8"x10.5". Square up now.

Step 8: Putting it All Together.

This is the fun part. You can decide where you want your cabin to be placed. I felt it would be more interesting off center, so I stitched four trees to the right of the cabin and 9 to the left. I had a whole other tree attached (hence my instructions for 14 trees) but I removed it, as the piece was about 4 or 5" longer than its spot on the MP. As mentioned, I quilted so much that the piece shrunk considerably and in hindsight I should have left it.

Once your trees and cabin strip is assembled, sew the black border to the top and the floral border to the bottom. The piece should measure 16"x57" (approximately with that 14th tree) This is the last section for the bottom of the quilt, and a fun print gives a nice finish. How sweet will this be hanging off the foot of the bed?

Step 9: The Quilting.

This is our biggest piece yet. You'll need to do a lot of ditching to stabilize the piece. You will be joining with a sashing strip so you can baste and quilt to all the edges. Before the perimeter basting, I went ahead and ditched the seams between both borders. This eliminates the extra puffing that can happen within 16"x55" of space between the basted edges. After the border ditching, I basted around the piece 1/8" from edges to stabilize. I then ditched the trees and every line of the cabin.

Free Motion Tree Blocks:

You can use the block keys given or use a transparency sheet to practice a few different quilting designs on top of your blocks. This time, I drew a few options in Sketchbook Pro on my ipad and came up with the following:

The doodling I did was very basic. Like Kindergarten. The beauty of the quilting will appear in the stitches themselves so the practice doesn't have to be pretty. Obviously.

Free Motion Cabin Block:

For the cabin, I sketched quickly and used the following quilt designs:

Again at Kindergarten. There is no right or wrong. Just play and have fun. It will be beautiful! My intention here is to show you my "real" way of designing quilting patterns. Nothing fancy. Nothing computerized. Nothing intimidating. Rather than give a CD with professional looking patterns that are hard to print from, I want this to be realistic for you. Look at my scribbles! You can do way better than that. The only thing you have to be willing to do is put in the time and design developing effort. You can do it!

Threads:

*The entire sky was done in one length of blue poly thread by Sulky for the sheen.
*I used a multi color Sulky cotton green thread on all the trees.
*Mettler cotton brown on both the ground fabrics.
*The floral was quilted with one continuous thread in Superior King Tut 40 multi color cotton.
*The "logs" of the cabin were stitched with a tan poly.
*The roof was done in dark brown Cotton Mettler.
*I ran three straight lines of black with my walking foot on the black border.

It's Too Short For the Main Piece!

My lack of interest in careful planning has caused me to get resourceful once again. This is an easy fix if you have fusible fleece. Since the section is quilted, we can't just sew on a front and back strip. We need some heft. You could spray baste a strip of batting on one of the strips, or even better, fuse on a strip of fleece outside the seam allowance on each piece and it will stay in place. This is how I add borders to a finished quilt when I want a more substantial frame than just the standard ½" binding. We will be finishing this quilt this way so I can show you.

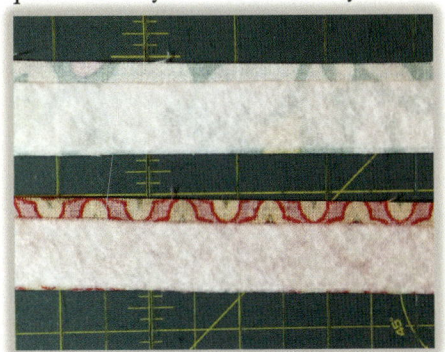

Since the piece is only ½" short (I was so close! Oh well. Quilt happens.) we'll need a 1" strip in each fabric for the back and front the same height as Section 11, which in our case is 15.5". Also, Cut 2 pieces of fleece ¾"x15.5" and fuse each to the WS of each piece leaving that ¼" seam allowance as shown above. Lay the back strip RS up on surface, align the raw edge of the side of the section you're joining on top of that strip with RS facing up (back fabrics will be facing each other), and then lay the front strip WS up so the front fabrics will face each other. Pin in place. Stitch a line along the fusible fleece and press both open so the fleece is facing each other. You can run a basting line on the outside to keep these together so they don't keep flapping open. There. Done!

I chose one of the outer fabrics of the log cabin to continue the line coming down the left side. I like to call that a design opportunity. After all, I don't make mistRakes.

Step 10: Attach With Sashing

Since I didn't quilt outside of the ½" joining space on the black border strip, we could add this to the MP without a sashing. But I felt like aesthetically it just needed a bit more detail or lightening up. I also have a feeling I'm going to want to do some embroidery on this black border later and will want another buffer between this section and the hexies.

I chose a black and white print sashing for the front. Join your Section 11 to the main piece with the sashing as per the instructions on page 39-40.

After joining, you may find the seam allowance is bulky. If so, it's okay to trim the seam allowance of one of the pieces so it fits better. This is especially true when using wool batting and heavy cotton or flannel. See above. It makes it a bit easier to hand stitch the ½" sashing across the front. And I'm all about making things a bit easier.

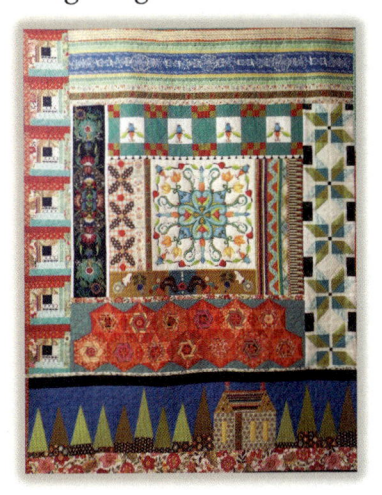

Quilt now measures 67.5"x53.25"

SECTION 12:
FABULOUS FUSIBLE FLORALS

While there is still a bit of debate in the quilting world whether using fusible web for applique is "cheating", it has pretty much become a mainstream practice by even the highest rank of pros and I couldn't be happier. While I love the look of turned edges, and admire the skill of those who master it, there are limits to the kinds of shapes one can create based on a quilter's own ability. And time! It is freeing to be able to creatively draw out your own shapes and transfer them to the fusible web, fuse them to chosen fabrics and artfully arrange them on a background without worrying how you're ever going to turn those crazy edges. Remember Colorforms? It's like that. Only permanent. Fusible and turned applique are two totally different art forms. So don't let anyone tell you that fusible applique is cheating. Because it isn't. It's awesome.

Materials:

Fabrics: Lots of scraps and leftovers for the applique pieces. For the backgrounds and borders, starting at the top:
8"x17" red print; two 8"x2" strips green for top /bottom borders; two 1.5"x20" aqua dot for sides
8"x7" yellow print; two 10"x2" strips olive dot for top/bottom borders; two 1.5"x7" red dot for sides
8"x11.5" aqua print; two 10"x2" strips ochre for top/bottom borders; two 1.5"x11.5" red dot for sides
8"x24" polka dot; two 8"x2" strips orange for top and bottom borders; two 1.5"x27" border print sides

Backing and Batting: 72"x12".

Fusible web: Steam A Seam II Lite is the best product on the market. You can reposition the pieces while you play with the arrangement as the product is tacky and they won't slide all over. There are other great products on the market and their uses vary with the techniques and fabrications you are working with. But in this case, get a few yards of Steam A Seam II Lite on the roll from your quilt shop. It comes in 8x11 packages which is fine too.

Drawing Pad, Sharpie and Scissors: For drawing and cutting template shapes out.

Step 1: Build Your Backgrounds

Each bordered panel is built separately then stitched together. Once you have your four panels, line them up next to the quilt, arrange in the order you like and sew them together to create a strip that will measure 10"x70."

For the red and polka dot sections, the top and bottom borders (sizes can be found under materials list) get sewn on first then the sides. The red section will measure 20" and the polka dot 27" unfinished.

For the yellow and aqua sections, the sides get sewn on first followed by the top and bottom borders. The yellow section measures 10" high and the aqua 14.5" unfinished.

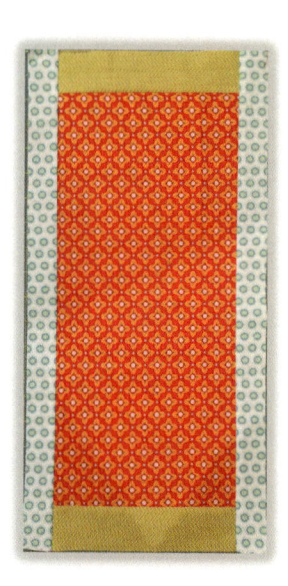

Beautiful canvas screaming for applique.

Step 2: The Quilting.

As you've probably figured out, I prefer to quilt the background before I add any applique or design elements. Unless you're going to have a quilt top long-armed or hand quilted, it just makes sense to me to avoid working so hard to stitch the background quilting in between the spaces of the motifs.

Once the piece is in one long strip, make sure you know what side you would like to attach to the MP. Flip and try both options. The quilt takes on a whole new look when it's flipped upside down (or right side up, as the case may be). Make the sandwich and pin in the corners and a few along the sides.

Ditch the seams that separate the individual blocks, being careful to stop ½" away from that joining side. Got your blue tape? Now ditch around the center panel of each block and again ½" outside the panel. You can run a basting line along the non-joining side now.

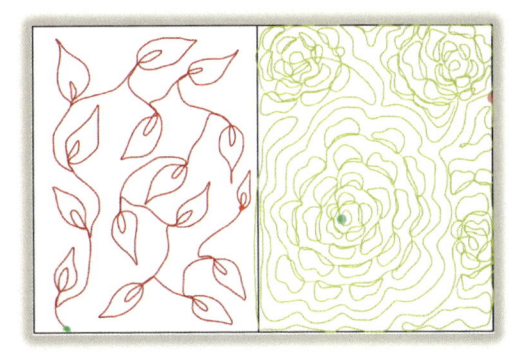

Above are the two quilting designs I drew out for the backgrounds of Section 12. I worked the leaves on both the aqua and red sections. Starting at the green dot in the lower left, work random vines and leaves with a teardrop detail. Travel back down the stem about ½" to start the next vine and leaf motif. This is done with one thread.

The cabbage rose motif was stitched on the yellow and the polka dot. Start at the green dot and work one petal at a time clockwise around the center and then around the previous petals of the flower in a spiral. This is also done with one thread. See my YouTube video for a demo on these.

Here is the position where I'm about to start a cabbage rose. Work a small circle to start, and then begin to work petal shapes with a curvy detail at the bottom of each petal around the circle. Keep going around clockwise stitching petals above the previous ones. When the flower is the desired size (in this case when the outer petals touch the 2 edges), work a curvy line about 5" away from the flower and stitch another flower. In the space between flowers, work meandering echo lines to fill in.

This motif is a bit more challenging than the leaf and stem line, so if you just feel like doing the easy leaves, you can do that. There is going to be so much work done on top with the applique, so don't spend too much time on the background.

Step 3: Put Pen to Paper/Gather Scraps

Grab a sketchpad and doodle shapes that you may want to try to make into applique. Inspiration can come from your fabrics, our natural world, copyright free books, and your own imagination. The sketches don't have to be perfect and no one has to see them.

Gather some of the leftover scraps of fabrics that you've used in this quilt. I chose a lot of solids, as my backgrounds were prints.

Once you have a design that appeals to you, draw it in the size you want on a heavier paper with a Sharpie. Take a phone photo for reference on placement, then cut them out on the line. These are your templates.

Rather than trying to make shapes on both sides of a motif match exactly, draw them on one side and use the reverse side for the mirror image template. Use the same templates many times. You are welcome to use my drawings. They'll have to be slightly enlarged to fit in your chosen panel. But it's even easier to draw them in your own hand.

My Pep Talk on Drawing

Most people assume they can't draw. I've even come across quite a few students who say they can't sketch or draw even though they have never even tried. This fear-based assumption comes directly from either an anxiety of other people judging their work or a classic fear of failure. First of all, no one needs to see your sketchbook or personal drawings. So there's that. And secondly, you're not going for a beautifully-shaded exact likeness of a subject that you're going to frame and hang in the foyer.

Keep in mind, there is no such thing as failure when it comes to drawing. Lose your expectations of the outcome and just doodle and enjoy the shapes you are making from your own mind. There is no way I will believe you if you say you cannot draw a teardrop, a heart, some leaves, a swoosh, a few different scrolls and a comma. That's all I have done and now have a great applique section. Once you gain confidence in simple shape drawing, play with the layout of the shapes. Cut them out and put them together in different ways and take photos to record the arrangements. Pick your favorite.

This is really fun. Let go of your fear. Spend some time with this. It's a worthwhile practice and the only way to gain confidence in your drawing ability. Let the dust bunnies grow. Leave the dishes in the sink. Put your iPad away. Do this, and your applique section is going to be amazing. You'll be so happy. I pinky swear.

Step 4: Make Fusible Shapes

Steam A Seam II Lite is a double-sided fusible web. You'll trace each WRONG SIDE of the templates onto the gridded side of the paper. Since most of our shapes are mirror images, you'll need to cut at least one of each side anyway. But it's a good idea to write R on the right side of each template and W on the wrong so you know what you're cutting.

Cut each shape out of the fusible and remove the non-marked paper side so that you can place the rough side of the shapes on your chosen fabrics (left). Press with a hot steamy iron for 5 to 10 seconds and let cool. Cut the fabric shapes along the lines and peel off paper. No need to add seam allowance since you're not turning.

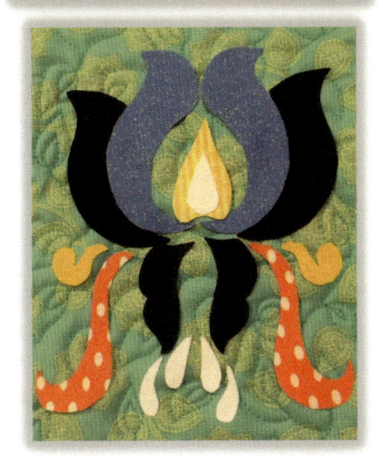

Loosely arrange the shapes back into the motif you originally drew onto your background and lightly hand press to temporarily hold in place. Set aside while you do the other 3 panels.

One simple leaf, 3 stems, circles and a couple of flower heads make a really great looking block. You don't need an art degree. I don't have one. I just like to doodle and play.

Save Your Hands

When I first started working with fusible applique, I discovered how much cutting is involved. Three times per shape can be a lot of wear and tear on the wrists. You can eliminate the middle step (of cutting fusible only) by ironing a square of Steam A Seam onto the fabric first, tracing the template directly onto the fused fabric and then cutting out the shape. The drawback of that is what seems like the waste of fabric. But if you're going to be doing a lot of fusing in the future, save those scraps as it's nice to have them when needing small shapes.

The other thing you can do to aid in the cutting process is get an Accuquilt cutter, or my favorite, the Brother CutNScan 550. It is one of the best quilting tools I've come across. It comes with lots of shapes and motifs specifically for quilting, and I also use it to draw my own shapes onto paper, scan them in, save the file and turn right around and program the machine to cut them in any size I choose. I don't have to cut the templates or the fusible. Instead, I only cut the motif once, which is the fabric step.

When doing turned applique, I'll cut the shapes out of my Apliquick fusible, press them to the WS of the fabric and cut them out with a loose ¼" seam allowance, getting them ready to turn. Again, once per shape.

Check these products out if you're planning on doing lots of applique. While not cheap, it is well worth the investment.

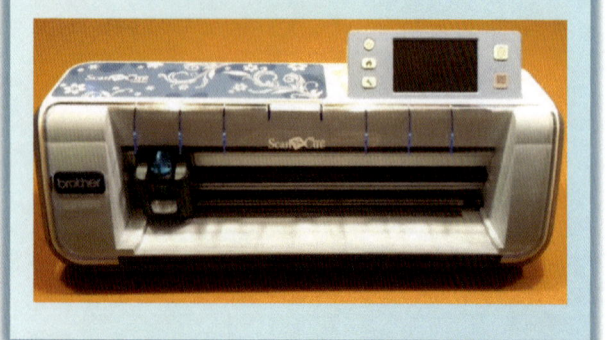

Step 5: Neaten Up and Press

When the backgrounds are filled with shapes to complete a pleasing mirror image symmetrical motif, find the center of the panel and straighten it all out. I used a ruler to find the exact center and then to check placement in a few places as I built out to the edges, but other than that, it was done by eye. I did no marking of the background panel itself. Using a hot steamy iron, press all the shapes in place. Don't run the iron back and forth, just press so you don't move the pieces out of line.

Step 6: Stitch it Down

It would be great if we could just leave the shapes as is and move on. But as you can see just by handling the quilt, the edges will start to shred and ravel by the end of the day. You've got a couple of options. If you don't want the stitching to show on the back, you'll need to hand stitch around each shape with the blanket (buttonhole) stitch. This is time consuming, but very relaxing. The other pros are you have much more control and can change colors much more easily than with machine stitching. Please see the instructions on page 31 in Section 3 where I demonstrated this stitch around the leaf. You can use a thread to match the applique or for more detail, use a contrasting color or even black to outline each shape. When I hand stitch, I like to use silk or poly. The sheen is beautiful.

This time I decided to stitch the shapes down with the applique stitch on my machine. This takes some patience, so if this is a new technique for you, please work on this with some extra similar shapes on your practice quilt sandwich first. It will be worth the time you spend.

Keep in mind, you will see the stitches on the back and you will be further quilting this section. I actually like the look of the buttonhole stitch on the WS of the quilt, so this is a plus for me. One other thing: This will save you time. But just barely. This is very slow machine work. **Don't rush through.**

I used black to outline all the shapes to coordinate with Section 1 where I worked in black for the quilted outlines. It's a bit risky because with black, every stitch shows, but I'm not a perfectionist so I went ahead with it. As I've said before, I always want to do my best work, but striving for perfection takes the joy right out of the process for me. Others revel in getting it just right and I respect that completely. Do what works for you and you'll have lots of fun.

If you want to do something other than black, try clear thread (with thinner thread in bobbin) or match your applique colors. Make sure you are practicing your chosen threads to see what it looks like on the WS of the quilt and that you're happy. You can also try a zigzag instead of the applique stitch. On your practice piece first, of course.

Back in Black
(if you're an AC/DC fan)

Step 7: Join.
Join Section 12 to the main piece without sashing as instructed on Page 25. Hand stitch the back and press. Square up. Mine measures 67.5"x62.5" at this point. One section left!

Hints for Successful Machine Applique:

Looking closely at the photo above, you can see a couple places where I have some disconnect with the black threads. This is very minor to me and hardly noticeable in this crazy busy quilt, so I did not take the stitches out to redo it. But I learned. This happened because I turned my fabric too sharply in the middle of the stitch set (see below). Here are the things to keep in mind as you machine applique:

1. Always have your needle in down position.

2. Know the stitch set. Mine is 5 stitches: Forward, Back, Forward, Left, Right. Repeat this in your head as you stitch like a mantra. Make turns with your fabric when needle is down in the "Right" position.

3. The forward back forward should run just outside the edge of the shape. The left and right actually hold the shape in place.

4. Auto knot at the end of each shape so your machine will start at the beginning of its set for the next shape.

5. Never turn your fabric while machine is stopped without lifting up the pressure foot first. It might seem like you can turn it slightly but when the machine starts again, you'll get a jog when the fabric straightens out.

6. Have the mindset that machine applique is saving just a small amount of time by not hand stitching. This is imperative. The picture to the right shows about an hour and a half worth of stitching. The amount of time it took to listen to Men in Black in the background. Come to think of it, some shapes look a bit alien, don't they?

SECTION 13:
TRIP AROUND THE WORLD.

Fitting right? I feel like I've taken a trip around the world with this quilt. And we're almost home. For this last section, I envisioned a linear top mimicking the larger squares in the quilt, using up some of the leftover fabrics and incorporating all the colors we've used to bring it all together. The trip around the world block is one of the easiest and most fun ways to play with color. Not just blocks, but whole quilts are made by working this technique.

Materials for Section 13:

Fabrics: Leftover fabrics from the quilt. We'll be cutting 3" squares so anything bigger than that.
Yarns: 5 different ribbon type yarns or actual ribbon.
Batting and Backing 65"14"
Sashing: 1"x63" backing; 1.5"x63" sashing (where I used teal)

Step 1: Cut Some Squares.

The best way to work with this block is to cut squares of a given size and arrange in different ways until you get a pleasing array. In our case, cut 3" squares of the fabrics we've used already.

Looking to the square on the right, start with a center square, of which you'll need just one. Then cut 4 squares out of a fabric that contrasts with the center (orange). The next fabric will surround the previous in a circle so you'll need 8 squares (green leaves). Cut 8 squares out of the next fabric (stripes). NOTE: if we were making this bigger, you would need 12 striped squares so you could put a square on top of each outer leaf to complete a circle. To end our 5-squares across block, cut 4 squares for the corners.

Be mindful of the direction your blocks are facing if you are cutting directional fabrics. They don't have to all go the same way, but you do want them symmetrical.

Step 2: Sew Squares into Strips.

Lay out the block grid as it will be when it's assembled. To keep track of the order while sewing, stack the squares into columns starting at the upper left hand corner and working down to the bottom row for each column. See above. This is the top row of each column.

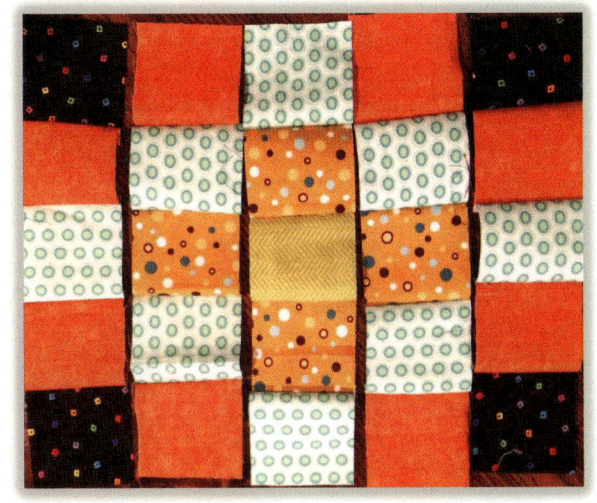

Sew into vertical strips and line them up as shown above. I didn't chain piece here. It takes too much time to reassemble for me. It's just as fast to just sew each piece to its neighbor. It is vital that you use the same ¼ seam allowance for each square. In other words, if you choose a scant (a bit less than ¼"), keep using the scant. Otherwise, the square seams won't line up nicely which can be slightly disheartening. Best to plan ahead.

For each strip, press the seam allowances to the left.

Step 3: Sew Strips into a Block.

Arrange your strips so that the seams of each next strip are pressed in the opposite directions as shown below. Since the strips are symmetrical, this is easily done.

Place three pins into the seams along the strip before you sew them together making sure that the seams of the opposite strips line up. (13" unfinished.) Make 5 blocks of different fabrics and then stitch the blocks together to make a 63" block strip set.

Step 4: Quilt and Couch

I decided to keep the quilting simple since there are so many different fabrics coming together and I intend on couching some yarns onto the piece to make the grid smaller

Make the quilt sandwich. Ditch each vertical and horizontal seam. We're going to join this section with sashing, so you can take the quilting to the edges. Choose 5 ribbons or ribbon yarns that coordinate. Lay a yarn out lengthwise in the middle row of the piece and "couch" over it with a contrasting thread. Couching simply means to secure the yarn with a zigzag stitch. Next couch a different yarn in the short center columns of each of the 5 blocks. Then do a different yarn lengthwise on either side of the first one and couch. Repeat until all sections have a yarn running through the middle of them. Join to the MP with sashing as seen on pages 39-40.

Finishing:
Frame Border

Congrats! You made a very large bed quilt (62.5"x79.5") on your domestic machine. A Bohemian artful piece that you and your loved ones will enjoy for years to come. Because it's all quilted, all you have to do is press it out, put a binding or a border on it and look at it as a whole to see if it might need some finishing touches. Doesn't that feel great!?

If you've made a quilt before, you may have done a traditional binding, which involves making an enormously long 2.25" strip to sew around the entire quilt. This would give us a .5" border and finish of the quilt beautifully. However, in this case I want a more substantial 1.25" black border to frame this complex piece. If you are happy working a traditional .5" binding, certainly feel free. The instructions for that are on pages 118-119 as that's how the Flowers on Courthouse Steps quilt is finished. If you want to try something a little different, try my frame border described here.

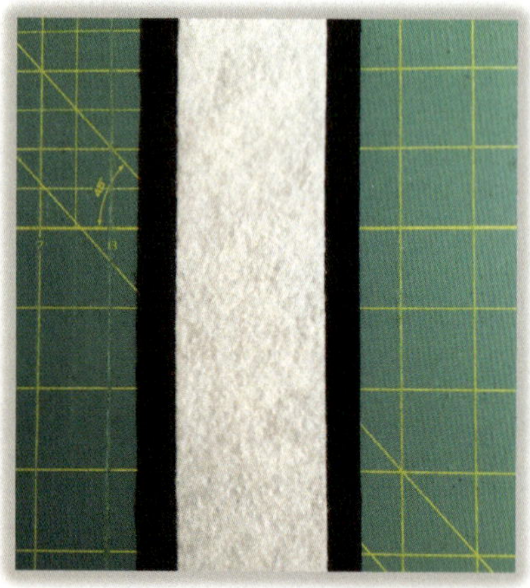

Start with the long 79.5" edges. Make two black strips 79.5"x3" and cut 2" wide fusible fleece strips long enough to cover the black strip. Fuse the fleece right down the middle of the black strip so you'll have ½" of fabric on each side. You'll need one and a half pieces of fusible off the bolt. *Press each long side in ¼" so the black raw edge butts up against the fusible.

Fold the piece in half lengthwise WS (fusible) together. This fold line is the outer edge of the quilt frame.

Line up a raw edge of strip with the raw edge of one longer side of the quilt and with a walking foot, stitch on the ¼" fold. Repeat for the other strip and long side. Hand stitch down in the back.

The width of the quilt now measures approximately 64.5." (Yours may be different and that's okay – simply follow these directions for your own measurements).

Cut two 3" top and bottom strips and piece to make strips 65.5." Cut 2" fusible fleece strips to cover the strips as before but leave ½" uncovered at the short ends. Begin by pressing each short end under ¼" twice. Then follow the instructions from the * above. When you stitch these to the tops and bottoms, incorporate the folded short ends into the stitching. When you go to hand sew the frame on the back, sew the short ends closed.

NOTE: I frame my art pieces this way quite often. I have mitered corners and even quilted the pieces before adding them to the MP. This takes a bit of mind-blowing math and patience, but it sure looks pretty when you get it right. If you find wood grained fabric and completed this method of finishing a quilt, it would look like a wooden frame. Play with this a bit on your next small art piece. Take notes on the mitering math so you can work larger more easily.

Reflection:
Looking at the Whole Picture

Now that the piece is finished and framed with a heavy black border, we can look at it from a distance to see if there are any places that might need a bit of tweaking. Although, the quilt as a whole is very busy, each section itself is a place for the eye to rest and for you to enjoy your craftsmanship. Take this opportunity to look away for a moment and then view the quilt again. Where does your eye go?

On my quilt, my eye goes right to the blue sky in the cabin and trees section. It needs stars to break up that solid color. The black sashing above it will get some repetitive embroidery, which was an idea I had during its construction. The only other thing that catches my eye is the white diamonds between the Nordic Star blocks. They are a little stark so I added embroidered wool circles.

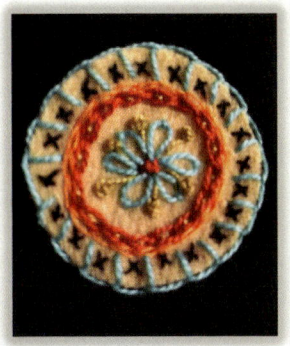

So how do you know when it's done? The answer will be different for each of us. I left mine hanging for a couple of days and would occasionally walk by it to see if some idea would pop into my head or if there was a bare place that called for more. I struggled a bit with the trip around the world section and thought that it may need organic shapes to tone down the graphic nature of it. But every fabric or stitch audition I considered looked too forced and over the top. So for me, when it gets to the point of trying too hard to enhance it, I listen to the quilt when it tells me it's finished.

And it is finished. I loved every minute of it and I hope you did too. Send pictures to me!

FLOWERS ON COURTHOUSE STEPS
66x93"

With this quilt, I wanted to stay a bit more traditional and focus more on patchwork and applique blocks as a foundation for some more intricate quilting. As we did in the Nordic quilt, we will be starting with a center square and building out from there. The difference here is that the two opposite sides will match each other and will be added to the main piece at the same time as when constructing a traditional courthouse step block.

Materials for Quilt:

Fabrics:
- 2 yards Bernartex Sundance Marble White cotton
- 2 yards solid black cotton
- Cherrywood Fabrics fat ¼ bundles in: Kiwi Berry and Dutch Tulip
- 1 yard Coordinating print: Jinny Beyer Milan RJR Fabrics
- 8.5 yds backing, borders and sashing : Moda Spirit/Lila Tueller
- 1/2 yard floral print for Broderie Perse Applique

Batting: 1/8" loft cotton by Mountain Mist Queen size
Threads: Aurafil for piecing and some quilting; Mettler for most quilting
Other: Apliquick glue/tools, Steam A Seam II Lite, Best Press, Freezer Paper

82

SECTION 1:
PATCHWORK TULIPS.

Constructing this block is another one of those times where we will use both the rotary cutter and templates. It also has y-seams, which are actually really fun and not as scary as you might have heard. Notice in the parallelogram patches that there is just one patch of fabric being used. To maximize the beauty of the Cherrywood (or other shaded) fabrics, I decided to strip piece shades of red and green and then make patches from the template. Also, I used a template for patch A so I could fussy cut from the fabric. Details will follow.

Materials:

Fabrics: fat quarters in Cherrywood: purple, 2 reds, 2 greens, white and Milan print
Back and batting: 22" square of each
Threads: Aurafil for piecing, and in bobbin during quilting to match colors of top. Mettler silk finish for quilting.
Template Plastic. Parallelogram template on next page.

Step 1: Precutting:

Cut two strips 2.5"x WOF from white for top A and C.
Cut two strips 2"x16.5" and two strips 2"x19.5" from Milan for borders around full block.

A: (bottom) cut 2.5" template from plastic
B: Cut two 5 3/16" squares from white
D and E: cut templates from plastic (next page).
F: Cut two 4 7/8" squares of purple.

Detailed instructions for each patch to follow.

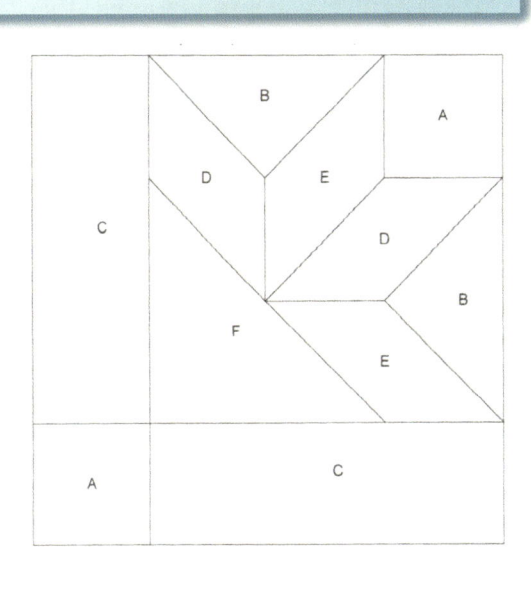

83

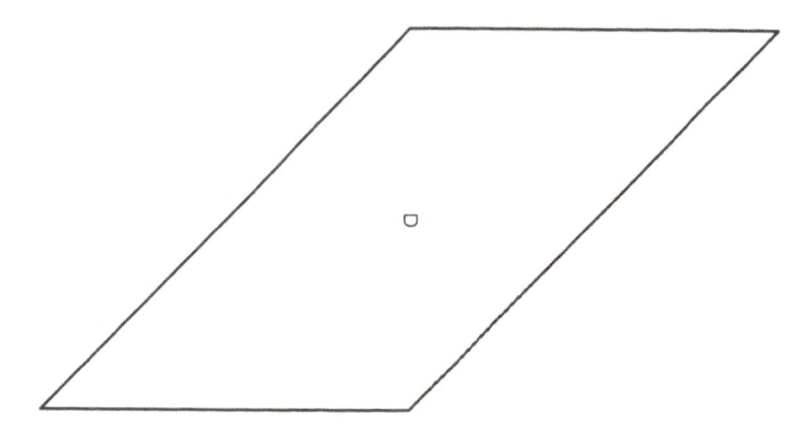

Trace the D/E template above out of template plastic and a sharpie. Cut it out on the line. If you're fussy cutting the center square, cut a 2.5" square out of the plastic as well. Don't mark on it yet.

Step 2: Fussy Cut Bottom Patch A

If you don't want to fussy cut the center patch, cut a 2.5" square out of the same purple as F, a shade darker or even a print. If you want to try to get a design in the center box when all the squares are put together, take the "A" template and place it on the print. Find a motif within the fabric you like.

When you find a good spot, use a Sharpie to mark shapes so that when you place the template on the fabric again, you can match it exactly. This step is important. Use a small rotary cutter to cut around the template. Cut straight down and forward rather than angled along the template, which will undoubtedly shave off the edges of the plastic.

When you get four squares cut out, play with the rotation to see which formation you like best. For mine, I actually like the left set better, but in this case, I chose the right since it is a better play for the bottom of the vase.

Step 3: Strip Piece Patches D and E

If you don't want shading, skip the following instructions and cut the patches out of a single solid fabric (include a ¼" seam allowance) using the template. Write D on front and E on back (E is the reverse). For the shading, draw a line on the front of the template ½" from the bottom long edge. Write "dark" on the narrow half.

You'll need a dark and light shade each of green and red. If using fat quarters, cut two 1" strips from the 22" side of the dark fabrics; and 1 3/8" from the 22" side of the light fabrics. If using yardage, one strip WOF of each is enough for all four blocks. Sew the long edges of the reds together and then the greens so you have two shaded long strips.

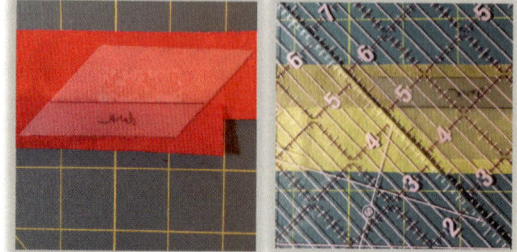

The strip is the correct height (including seam allowance) so all you have to do is run the template along the strip and cut the short ends with a ¼" seam allowance on each end. For four blocks, cut 16 total patches: four each of two colors in both the front (D) and reverse (E) cuts. Line up the drawn line with the seam making sure the word dark is on the dark fabric. Use double sided tape to hold in place. Don't flip the template after each cut to get alternate Ds and Es. Instead, cut four patches of D, then flip the template over and cut the four E patches to save on fabric.

Step 4: Rotary Cut the Rest.

Cut four 2.5" pieces from the white strips for the top A patch and eight 6.5" pieces from the white strips for the C patches.

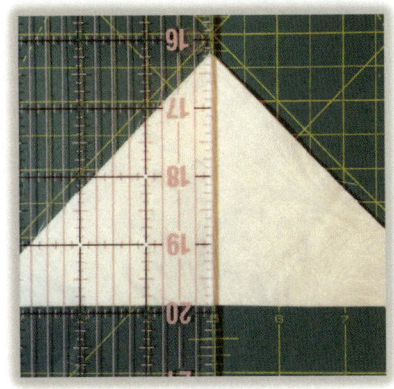

From the two 5 3/16" squares, cut twice diagonally. Cutting once will give you triangles. For the second cut, set up as shown above. When cutting on the diagonal, line up the square or triangles on the rotary mat and then make sure the ruler is straight with the edge running along the point(s) and then make your slice. In this case with unit B, you'll have 8 patches, enough for 4 blocks.

A measurement in eighths or especially sixteenths is tiny. Find the nearest fourth on the ruler and then slide it over just enough in the direction you need so the left fabric edge runs along the appropriate line. This works best if you place the ruler as shown below and use the marks on the ruler rather than the mat. If you are left handed, the opposite would be true. Remember the golden rule. Measure twice, cut once. Take your time. There are no extra points for speed. ☺

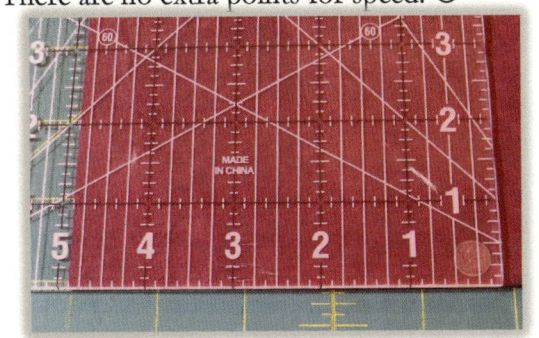

Out of the two 4 7/8" squares, cut once diagonally so you get four patches, which is enough for four blocks.

Step 5: Assemble the Block.

Lay out the pieces as shown in the way they would be put together to keep organized.

We'll start by assembling the eight (2 on each block) BDE sections together first. If you look at the block with the point at the bottom, there is a left and a right BDE section on either side of the white A square at the top. Let's do the left units first.

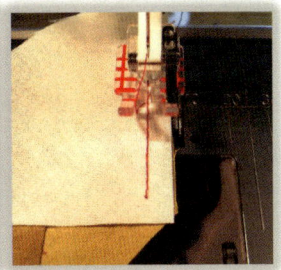

The secret to constructing a Y-seam is placing a dot on the WS of the B fabric ¼" away from the point and the two edges of the V and not ever stitching past it.

Mark all B pieces with a dot as described above. Place D and B RS together so that the long edge of B matches with the short edge of D. Flip over so the white triangle is facing up and you can see the dot. Start at the opposite edge and stitch your way down to the dot and knot and tie off as shown. Finger press to green side. Line up the E so the same edges match along the long side of the B patch. Flip so the dot shows and with the hand wheel, start and knot at the dot and stitch to the edge. Finger press to the red side.

Fold the unit so that it collapses into the shape of the D patch. The B triangle will actually fold up so that a little bit of it will peek out of the point. This feels like origami.

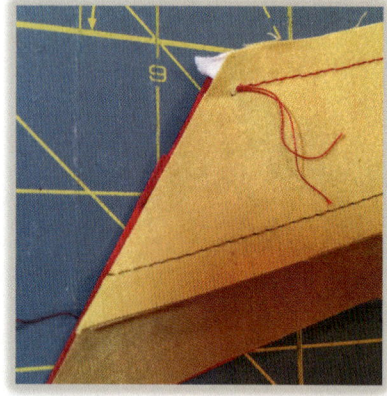

Starting at the dot, knot and stitch the diagonal seam down to the edges. Open up and finger press to the red. Run an iron from the long edge of B down to the point.

Flip and press. Or shall I say Presto!

Cut all the dog ears and threads and repeat the steps again until all 8 BDE units are made and you have a wonderful pile of four blocks that look like this:

Time to sew the top square in. You can start with either side. This is another y-seam. Make your dot at the corner of the square that will meet in the middle and stitch the first side to the dot, then the next side from the dot. Origami fold the piece and stitch from the dot down to the edge on the reds.

Press from the base of the tulip up to the white square. Leave all the seams that face down the way they are. Press the side tulip seam to one side and the top seam of the tulip to the point. This will reduce bulk in the block. When in doubt of how to press seams, give it a tug. They'll usually tell you which way they want to lay.

86

Now you're on easy street. Line up the RS of the F patch with the RS of the leaves so that you have dog ears sticking out equally of both sides and the base of the vase point lines up with the point of the top white square. The point will overlap it a bit. Stitch it on, press to the vase, clip the ears.

This square should measure 6.5" – trim and straighten the edges of all of them now. Sew the white 6.5" strip C to the right of each block. *Hint: stitch with the seams of the tulip block facing up so you don't cut off any points with the stitch line.* Sew the small base square (A) to the short end of the other white strip (C) being mindful of the fussy cut direction you chose. Line that to the left side of the tulip. To get the square A accurately placed, put a pin at the intersection where the square point meets the vase point. Stitch it down. Clip all threads (or they'll show through the white fabric) and press it out. This block will measure 8.5." Trim and square them all up.

Sew two sets of blocks together side by side. Again place pins in the vase patches. White shows every missed seam line. Then sew the halves together. Press mid seam open. Take the two 2"x16.5" border strips and stitch them onto the top and bottom; and then stitch the 19.5" borders to the sides. Press to borders. Trim and square up the block to 19.5."

Time for the quilting. Gulp. But fear not. There are lots of wonderful options for this block. Remember that there is no right or wrong way to quilt this. You can experiment with different motifs that you've learned or would like to try. Import the photo into your iPad or even print a few hard copies of your block and draw directly on them. Also, remember the clear film and Sharpie to draw right over your block. Be careful to use tape so it doesn't slip off and you mark your quilt! Of course, you can always follow my lead on the quilting patterns if you like what I've done.

I'm going for a mix of traditional quilting with a bit of free motion in color because I just can't help myself. I want to bring in some of the organic shapes of the border print with different colors of thread. However, I'm going to try my best to keep mostly with white thread on the white background because I so love that traditional textural look. Go ahead now and make your quilt sandwich with a 22" square of your backing and batting. Smooth it all out with your hands or even a dry iron and pin the corners. No need to baste as you're going to start by ditching the borders. See next page for details.

Step 5: Quilting the Center Block

Ditching is important to stabilize the block and also to set the tulips and vases up so they have their own puffy playing field, so to speak. This will help you get more familiar with the block under the needle and ideas may just start popping up when you least expect it. It sounds a bit metaphysical, but it really does work. Plus ditching is safe and easy. Not a lot of decision making yet.

Start by ditching the outer border seams and around the center square (not the seams within the square) with a thin white or clear thread and your walking foot. A walking foot helps keep the sewing line straighter and allows all the fabrics to run through the machine at the same pace.

Ditch the vases with purple, the leaves with green and the tulip heads with red. I didn't ditch the center white seams nor the shading within the leaves or flowers as I wanted them to appear as their own unit. While your walking foot is still attached, let's do the linear quilting. Break out your template plastic and Frixion or chalk pen for marking.

If you look closely, you can see a triangle shape of template plastic on the left half. To get your shape, place a piece of plastic big enough to cover the area you want to quilt and with a sharpie draw a sloping triangle as shown here. Cut it out on the line. This becomes your template for all 4 sections outside the center square. Just flip the template to the reverse to get the correct mirror image on the right side of the seam line. Make another triangle same shape but a bit bigger for echoing.

I did a set of sloping triangles that met at each corner of the center square so I could quilt both lines with one thread. Mark them:

Start at a corner and quilt them. Piggyback on the center square to get yourself to a seamline and stitch a line up to the point to start the echo lines within the diamonds:

You don't need to mark these lines. Find a spot on your walking foot to sew along to keep consistent widths between the lines. For mine, I keep the previous line somewhere in the open rectangles of my foot.

Work all the way around the inner diamond shape, piggybacking along the inner diamond to travel between the lines. When approaching the center seamline, try to work it so that you hit that seam just right. It's okay if the spaces vary slightly. Mine are within 1/8" differences. It makes it more interesting if they're not perfect. Really.

When the inner diamond quilting lines were completed, I took those sloping triangle templates and marked the angles about and inch and a half above the inner diamond. I also continued the linear pattern on either side of the tulip. Note that before quilting those tulip echo lines, I ran a curved line to outline each space.

Now that the linear quilting is done, you can change to your free motion foot and setup on your machine. In the large white negative space behind the outer diamond, I worked upside down stacked teardrop shapes to fill. With black, I worked pebbles in the center square.

Time to thread play and get color on the flowers.

Using template plastic, I drew a potential organic design to bring in some of the design from the print. You can't really trace this onto your fabric as it's now a quilt, so use chalk pencil or a Frixion pen to free hand draw this. If you're inclined to panic over drawing, just remember to break it down and draw one shape at a time. Start with the flame shapes, then outer scrolls, then the circles. And the other safety net you have is that you can simply erase the line you drew if you don't like it and start again. Careful with those Frixion pens on darker fabrics. You will get a very faint white residue. This will wash out eventually so I don't let it bother me.

Looking at the green patches, free hand draw some long leaf shapes and on the red, draw some elongated scrolling shapes to give a bit of texture. I also took the flame scroll circle shape up into the mouth of the tulip. Note how I didn't match threads to the fabrics in all cases. Play with this to see what you like. When all the quilting was done, I filled in some of the quilted shapes with thread painting different colors. Refer to the photo at the beginning of this section to see the completed quilting of the center block. You can do this!

The square is now 19" after quilt shrinkage. Trim and square it up.

SECTION 2:
BLENDED ANGLES.

Again, if you're using Cherrywood fabrics or other analogous solids that shade into each other, you want to maximize that effect by going from light to dark in either direction. I chose to use light in the center and work out to dark so that when the squares were assembled, it would create a nice border around the first section. You will be constructing 4 of these 2-block units in this section: two for Section 2 and two to set aside for Section 3.

Materials:

Fabrics: Cherrywood Fat Quarters in orange, orange yellow and yellow for angles
Bernartex ½ yard Sundance Marble for white background
Two 1.5"x20" backing fabric for border
Backing and Batting: Two pieces each 21"x12"
Threads: Mettler for top, Aurafil for piecing and bobbin

Cutting from Fat Quarters.

Since we'll be using eight blocks to complete both Sections 2 and 3, we'll go ahead and make all of them at once to save time. For now we'll be setting aside four of them for section 3 and using four to complete the two sides of Section 2.

Also, since I am (and imagine you may be) using fat quarters, I'm going to give exact strip measurements for each color to be sewn together. If we were using WOF strips, we could sew the length of them together first and then make length cuts to save time, but in this case I want to maximize every inch of my beautiful and expensive fabric that I don't have very much of. It's the right choice to spend a bit more on time and save on fabric.

Step 1: Strip Cutting:

Large White Triangles: Cut four 10 3/8" squares;
  Then cut once diagonally.
Small White Triangles: Cut four 3 ¼" squares;
  Then cut once diagonally.

From the 18" edge of fat quarter cut 2 3/16" strips:
Orange (outer) Strip: Cut 8 pieces: 2 3/16"x14 5/8"
Orange yellow (middle): Cut 8 pieces: 2 3/16"x11 ¼"
Yellow (inner) Strip: Cut 8 pieces: 2 3/16"x7 15/16"
  NOTE: You'll get 2 yellow strips from one 2 3/16"

On each colored strip, line up the piece so it runs straight along a mat line then hold up a ruler edge at 45" angle and make a slice. Make sure each end is sliced at mirror image angles rather than parallel. In other words, the lines would come to a point if they kept going up.

90

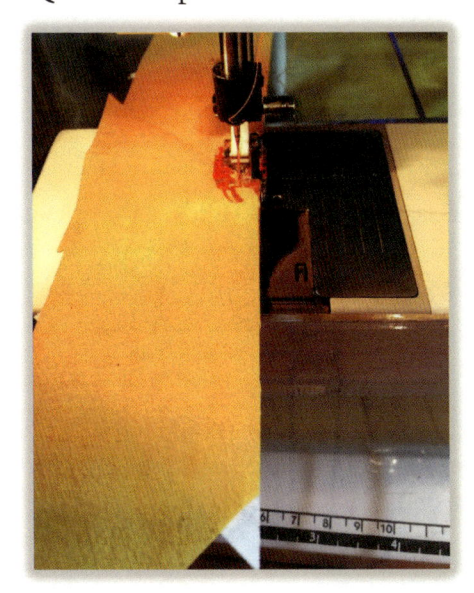

Step 2: Assemble and Combine Blocks.

Starting with the small white triangles, chain piece all 8 blocks in an assembly line. In other words, sew all the yellows to the whites as shown, then continue with all the yellow-orange strips, the orange and lastly, the large white triangles.

Don't worry about pressing until they're all sewn up. Then press the seams to the darker fabrics. These blocks should measure 10" so trim and square up to get there.

You'll be sewing 2 blocks together so the colors form a V. Place a few pins along the color seam lines and stitch the 4 pairs together. The inner V is the joining side. To 2 of them, add a 1.5"x20" strip of the backing fabric (trim excess). Set aside two of the block pairs for Section 3.

Step 3: Quilting of Section 2

Make your two quilt sandwiches. You'll be quilting both sections at the same time. With your walking foot, baste the non-joining long side 1/8" from edge. Ditch the sashing seam and all seams separating the colors with a thin thread in like-colors to the fabrics. Run an additional stitching line ¼" away from the seam onto the sashing strip to further secure.

Time for the fun part. Filling the colors in with quilting stitches. We will be bringing some of the straight line quilting used in the first section up into this one so don't remove your walking foot just yet. Here is my initial design drawn on the Sketchbook Pro app.

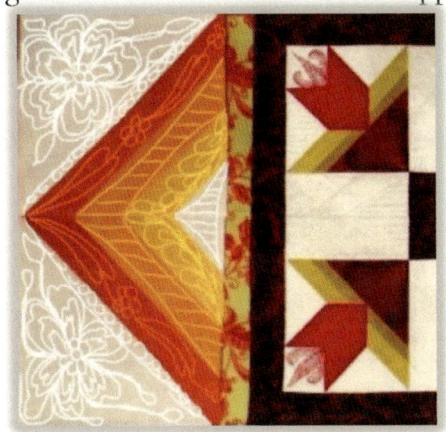

Not a careful precise drawing, but it give me enough of an idea to proceed. That's all you need to get a visual so doodle and draw!

I've echoed the linear pattern in the inner white triangles and the middle color stripe. With my walking foot still attached, I ran a shallow arc line just outside the outer color border (not shown in photo below).

Attach your free motion foot. I didn't mark any of the lines for any of the Section 2 quilting, but I wanted the leaf shapes to fall in the approximate spot on each side so I placed a ruler straight across the block and I marked at 2" apart then 8" apart:

In most cases, reference marks and a few gridlines are sufficient for free motion quilting, instead of marking the entire design.

After marking the dots on the outer orange strip, I quilted the shapes I drew in Sketchbook starting at the point and working down for each side with orange Mettler thread.

For the yellow strips, with yellow Mettler, I worked arched feathers starting at the bottom working up so that the tops curved up and met at the point. Inside each feather bump, I worked a teardrop shape for additional texture.

In the white large triangles, I started in the approximate center of the triangle and worked a 6 multi-layered petal flower. Coming out from each space between the petals, I stitched a vine with curly Qs and a leaf shape at each end. Each large triangle motif was done with the same thread, overlapping, making vines and piggybacking when needed.

It's almost done. I want to finish it off with a bit of contrasting colored thread in a few places as we did in Section 1. Looking at the piece above, the white areas on either side of the point of the triangle need some quilting. So I worked a yellow-orange arched feather on either side and then with the same thread, echoed and added scrolling vines to the orange quilting in the outer strip.

In the yellow feathers, I added a white stem that branches out into each feather bump. With a thinner Aurafil yellow thread, I made tiny circles inside the little arc line just outside the triangle. Don't attempt tiny circles or micro quilting with Mettler. It's too thick and you'll have a clumpy mess. Delicate quilting needs delicate threads. It's a great rule of thumb to remember.

Step 4: Trimming the Sections.
Since the joining sides are meant to be symmetrical, we need to trim these up as precisely as we can so they match and look straight. Give your wonky quilted sections a good steamy press to get them as flat as you can. We'll trim the joining side first.

Looking at the picture on the left, line your ruler up so the 1" line is running along the sashing seam. Take your Frixion pen and draw a line at the edge of your ruler. Fold back the batting and backing and with scissors, cut directly on the line (TOP only) to square up. Do this for both.

You may notice that the sashing has shrunk and that in some places, there is hardly any fabric at all to cut away as the more quilting in a particular spot, the more scrunched up the piece will be. Totally normal.

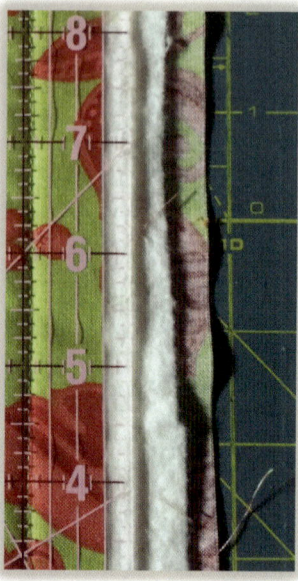

Looking at the picture on the right, with the piecing laying flat on the mat and backing and batting showing, place your ruler so that the ¼" line is on your cut and slice away the excess back and bat, leaving the required extended ¼" of each.

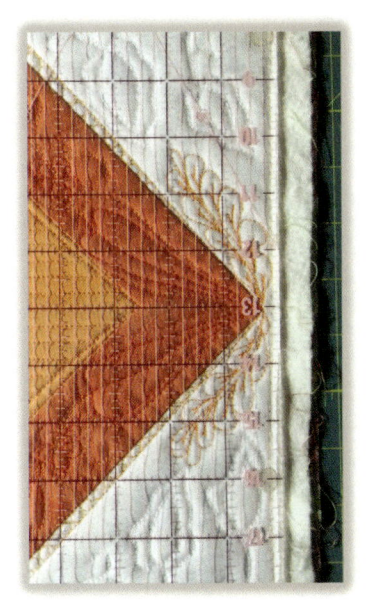

Once the joining sides are cut, place that edge on a vertical line on your mat. Now you can square up the other long sides. They should be relatively straight since the quilting was pretty even across the pieces. Make sure you don't slice off that ¼" of space above the point – you don't want to lose that when you join the next section! Mine now measure 10 ¾" tall.

Turn the piece so that the bottom and top lines line up with horizontal lines on your mat and slice off the extra back and bat on the short ends so they measure just over 19." Rather than cutting the piece to exactly 19" as we did in the Nordic quilt, here it's best to leave a bit extra to trim off after the piece is joined as you have two identical pieces you are trying to match up. Keep the point of the triangle in the middle of the piece. That is easier done with a little extra side fabric that you can manipulate later.

Step 5: Joining Sections 2.

The only difference between the joining here and the log cabin quilt is that you have two identical pieces that will be attached to the opposite sides of the center square. The actual joining is done the exact same way.

Place Section 2 on top of Section 1 RS together and make sure the point of the square lines up with the center seam of the blocks in Section 1. Fold back the back and bat and pin the top to the 3 layers of section 1 in place. Sew sections together with a ¼" seam, removing pins as you come to them.

Pin the back fabric back to keep it out of the way while you trim the batting. Press the seam just sewn from the back to get it flat.

Take scissors and EVER so carefully trim the batting so that the edge of it matches the batting from section 1 while laying down. In a perfect world, this bit of batting snuggles right in the space created by the 1/4" seam allowed for the joining and trimming.

With your iron, press down the batting, and trim any place it overlaps with the other. Fold the backing fabric under so the fold extends just past the seam you sewed to join the piece and hand applique in place.

SECTION 3: LIKE SECTION 2 ONLY BETTER
HEAT TURNED HAND APPLIQUE

Although the layout of the quilt is constructed like a courthouse step block, you're getting a little taste of assembling a medallion quilt where you would need to match 4 sides. And with the unpredictability of the sizing after quilting, it can be a bit tricky. There are a few hints and things to watch for that I'll discuss in this section to match everything up as much as possible. We can get really close on our lines and it will be beautiful.

Materials.

Fabrics: blocks made in previous section.
4 squares of white 10"x11.25"
Back or sashing fabric: two strips 1.5"x41" and four strips 10"x1.25"
Fat quarter pieces of 3 greens, 2 reds, 2 purples, 1 orange, 1 yellow.

Backing/Batting: two each of 12"x43"

Templates: Provided for flowers; 9" circle – I used an embroidery hoop

Turned Applique Kit: Small craft iron, Best Press or starch, Hera marker, freezer paper

Step 1: Build the Backgrounds.

Sew a white square onto each end of the block pairs you assembled in Sections 2. Then stitch on a backing or sashing strip to the entire joining side of Sections 3. Whatever sashing fabric you choose, make sure it is the same as what you used in Section 2. You may be wondering right now about that extra vertical sashing strip between the applique background and the V blocks. We could have certainly sewn that in now, but a better way to ensure the line up is to applique it on when the entire Section is done, quilted and assembled onto the piece.

FYI: Notice from the photo that I had to curve my sashing strips a bit to get it to line up. Yours will work better than mine with the Section 2 instructions. I stitched a line on the sashing strip further away than the instructed ¼" and as a result had to cut off more of the edge than I wanted to. Rest assured, the instructions have been altered for your success.

Again, I am designing this piece as I write, so I am learning as I go. But in showing and discussing my mistakes and pitfalls, my hope is that we both learn from them. What's that they say? The best way to learn something is to teach it to someone else.

Step 2: Quilting the Backgrounds

Since my quilting journey began a short time ago, I have been wondering why a person didn't machine quilt the background of a block BEFORE placing any applique, particularly if the design is linear. But I know now that I come to quilting from a different mindset than most people. With a case of the lazies and a bit of innovation, I choose the path of least resistance to execute the vision, rather than follow conventional methods. That's me in a nutshell.

Most people I know send out their quilts so I imagine a longarmer could more easily work around the shapes than those of us who are stitching big quilts with domestic machines. But with my method of quilt making, it is a no brainer to quilt these sections first and then add the fun stuff. Not that quilting isn't part of the fun!

For most of the quilting of Section 3, you don't have to think. This is a great opportunity to practice more of what you did in Section 2. Ditch all the places you worked previously. Run a ¼" line on the sashing strip. Ditch the seam that separates the white applique background squares to secure them. Go ahead now and repeat all the quilting you did in Section 2 for both pieces of Section 3.

On the white squares, place an approximate 9" circular template and with a Frixion pen, draw the circle. I traced the inside of the hoop. You could also use a pie plate, print a 8.5" circle out of paper, etc. When tracing, keep in mind that we need to leave more space at short ends for trimming. Stay ½" away from the ditch line for sashing space and center it between the sashing line and the outer edge less its ¼" seam allowance.

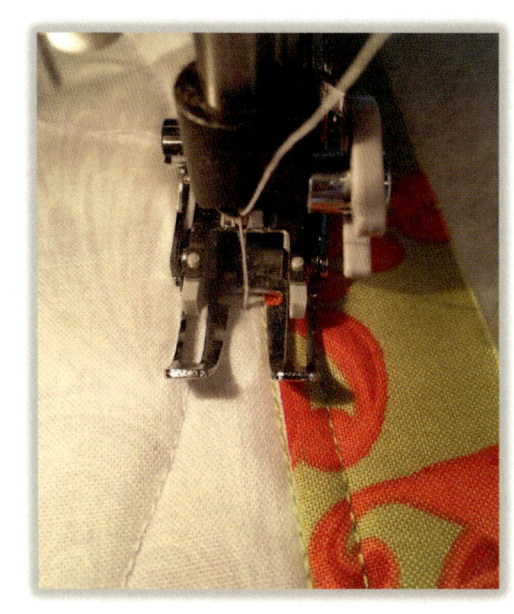

Stitch the line you drew with a walking foot and then echo it ¼" outside the line using your walking foot as a guide. Cut the first and use a second thread so you don't cross the spaces between.

I love the juxtaposition of a linear background behind organic shapes of applique. With a Frixion pen and a ruler held parallel to the outer edge of the triangle, draw one line at the inner edge of the circle. Stitch that line and use a guide on your walking foot to continue stitching lines ¼" apart. When you reach the end of each line, rotate the quilt slightly to piggyback on the inner circle. It will take 3-6 stitches up the side to get to the next line depending on where you are in the circle.

When you complete all the lines, end and weave in the thread. Draw a cross line at the inner edge of the circle at a 45 degree angle to the stitched lines and then stitch the cross grid. Work free motion feather loops outside the circle to fill the space.

Step 3: Heat-Turned Applique.
This is very similar to the method of glue turned edges that we did on page 30. Since the pieces are stacked on top of each other in this case, we can eliminate the extra bulk by using freezer paper instead of fusible web.

You'll need starch or Best Press poured or sprayed into a container (note my orange plastic margarita shaker) and a small acrylic flat head paintbrush. The craft iron shown below is incredibly helpful. You can use a small iron, but the ease of turning edges is ten times better with one of these. I love my Apliquick tools for turning with glue, but a Hera marker works even better with starch as it holds a bigger area and you have to work fast. You'll also need sharp small scissors, freezer paper and a Sharpie marker.

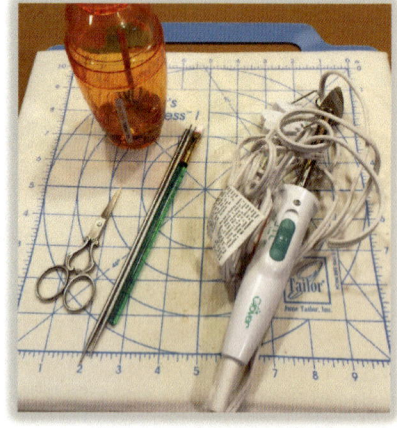

Heat up your iron and trace all the template pieces on the following pages on the SHINY side of the freezer paper so you get the reverse template.

This is standard procedure when doing freezer paper applique, but in our case it's a symmetrical design, so it doesn't matter which side you trace on. For times when it matters, remember to trace on the shiny side.

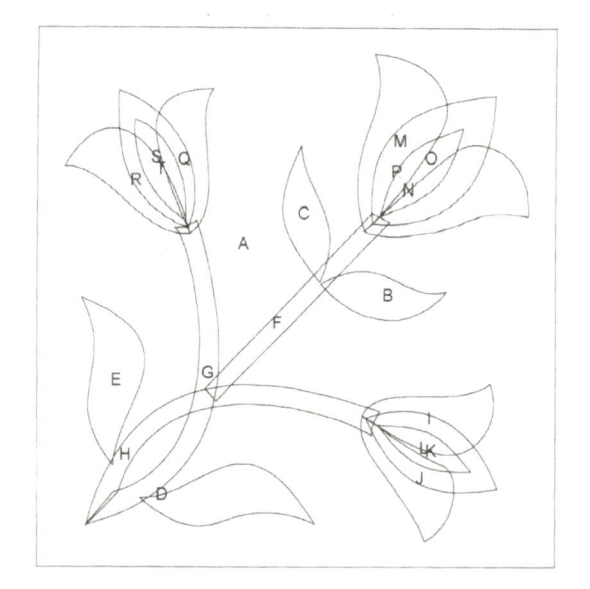

Turn each template over and label with its corresponding letter. Each shape above has its own template as you can't use the reverse of a template when using freezer paper since we need a shiny side for each. They can all be used 4-6 times. Note how the paper side of the template is the reverse of the shapes in the key.

Carefully cut each shape out just inside the drawn line. You don't want Sharpie getting transferred to fabric. I've never had this happen, just being safe.

Choose a fabric for each shape and use the iron to adhere each removable template to the WS of the fabric. Cut out each shape with a ¼" seam allowance. Don't remove the freezer paper yet. You will be turning around the edges. Clip slits into the inward curves close but not all the way to the paper. Clip fabric ¼" away from and straight across each point. Lay them out to make sure you have every piece accounted for and know where they all go. This will help you get familiar with the layout.

Below are the leaf and stem templates. I chose 3 different greens, but of course you can decide on whatever you want with what you have. If you choose a print, make it a small one. Also, you can use tone on tone or batiks. You'll turn every edge of every piece of the flowers and leaves except for both the short edges of the F stem and the straight edges of G and H stems as they get tucked under. You will be turning the angled ends of G and H. Also F is about an inch or two too long, so you'll be cutting off some of the length when placing applique layout later.

The tulip parts are on the next page. You can refer to the picture at the start of this section to see what I chose and go from there. Use copies of the key on the opposite page to try color combos.

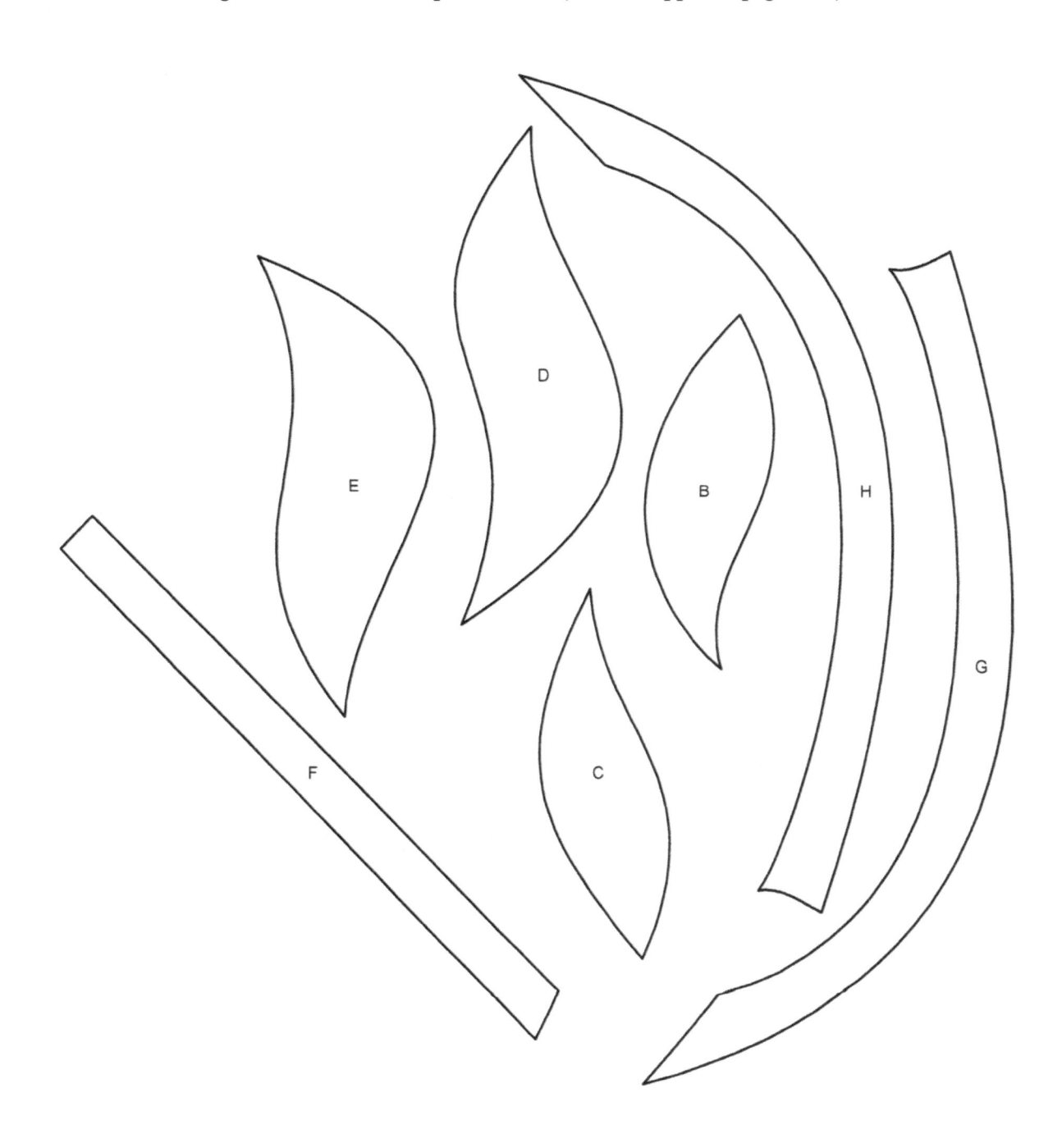

98

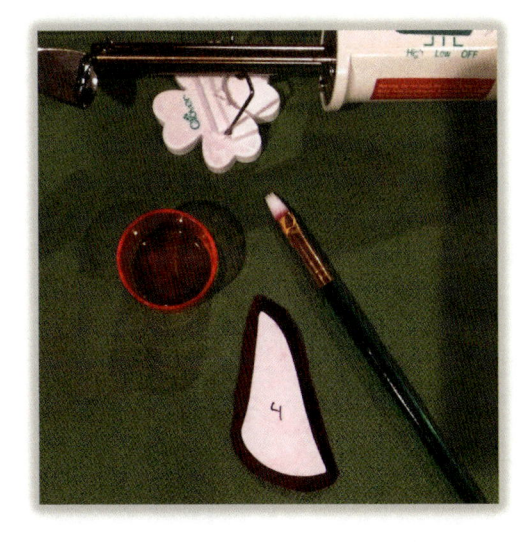

Start by placing a tea towel over your pressing surface to absorb the extra starch. I'm right handed so flip the instructions if you're left, as I know you are used to that. In photo 1, I'm ready to turn the easy top edge of the piece so place it on your workspace as shown. Dip your brush in the starch and "paint" a line down the seam allowance next to the paper. While starch is still wet, place the Hera marker to the edge of the paper (where it meets the fabric) to hold down the piece and use the hot iron as a wand to turn the entire edge onto the marker and then onto the paper. Flip piece around to work other side. See photo 2.

This side has a large curve that we need to address. Paint the seam allowance with starch and start with the deepest part of the bump as shown in photo 3. Take tiny presses close to the paper with the iron and work your way to the top and then down to the bottom of the edge. See my YouTube video on turning applique edges. If there is overlap at the points, fold back the tips as shown in the pressed applique pieces in Section 2 of the Nordic quilt, page 23.

Once all pieces are turned, carefully remove the paper and lay out as shown. Repeat the process 3 times. Get some good material to watch on TV or visit your Audible library. This takes 2 full days.

Step 4: Hand applique

Once you have all the pieces for all four blocks turned under, pin the centers in place (or place with small dabs of glue in the seam allowance staying away from the points). Watch the top and inner sides of the sections: make sure the red tulip shape is below ¼" or it will get chopped off in joining. Also, keep in mind that you will be appliqueing a sashing strip over the seams joining the white squares to the blocks so stay ½" away from that seam if you can. In addition, 1" of the outer edges will be chopped off after joining.

Center the entire design within the circle. The F straight stem was way too long for the block so I cut almost a full inch off the top. Don't worry about the seams opening up a bit and showing. You'll be hand stitching so you can "needle turn" them as you go. With the pressed seams, this is much easier than the traditional needle-turn applique technique.

Stitch each piece down with a matching thread to the applique (not the background). I started with the stems and leaves and then worked the flowers from the back petals coming forward.

Once the design is stitched down, you can hold it up to the opposite section and match it up as shown to the left. Get close. Don't pull your hair out.

After all the sections are stitched, you can press it with a hot steamy iron from the back and a quick press on the front.

Step 5: Quilt Details onto the Applique.

You can leave the applique unstitched as it should be secure enough without additional quilting. I love the look of unquilted applique, but in this case, wanted to add the extra texture in keeping with the quilting I've done so far.

I didn't go too crazy – I stitched an echo line the inside of the shapes with coordinating thread on the leaves and stems. On the flower heads, I ran a couple of lines following the shapes to give them texture.

Step 6: Trim and Join the Sections.

Follow the directions on pages 92-93 for trimming and joining of the sections to the MP. Line up the point of the triangle to the center seam of the Section 1 block as before. The other line to match up is the seam line between the applique section with the ¼" seam lines on the sashing of Section 1:

Pin, or even better, Wonderclip the Section in place so you can more easily open it up and check that it's aligned before stitching it on:

Once the section is stitched on, trim up the short ends so the quilt is squared up.

Fold under one short end of each of the strips At each seam line, center a strip over the seam and machine stitch a line down the center. Fold under the long ends so that the strip matches the sashing of Section 2 and makes a continuous line. Hand applique in place on both sides.

The piece measures 39" square. The next sections will be added to the adjacent sides. In other words, if Section 3 is at the top and bottom, Section 4 will get added to the left and right of the MP which would be in keeping with the construction of a traditional courthouse step block. Since the sides all look the same in this case, place a couple of Wonderclips or safety pins on the sides you're going to be working with for easy reference.

SECTION 4: SUGAR BOWL BLOCKS
BRODERIE PERSE

This section is fast and fun. The basic sugar bowl block is simple to put together and a great opportunity to fussy cut a square of fabric or work Broderie Perse, which means fussy cutting a motif out of a fabric and fusing it to the background. The white diamonds that result when the squares are put together will echo the large orange square shape in the center and the bold colors surrounding it will give a nice border to all that white. And it's all I can do to leave that white alone. As much as I love the simplicity of white on white quilting, as an artist, I see a blank canvas to stitch, paint or add other fibers to. But sometimes, as in this case, less is more. Learning how to edit is a big part of the creating process. A good design can be very simple.

Materials:

Fabrics: 1/3 yard white background; fat quarter pieces of four solid colors; flower print fabric for fussy cutting.
Backing/Batting: two 42"x10" of each;
Backing for Sashing: two 1"xWOF; two 1.5xWOF" strips for sashing; four 1"xWOF for 2 sides of Sections 3
Fusible: Steam a Seam 2 Lite for applique; fusible fleece .5"x39" strips for 2 sides of Sections 3.
Threads: Aurafil for piecing; Mettler white, red, purple

Step 1: Cutting and Sewing For Ten Blocks

Cut ten 6 3/16" white center squares
Cut five 5 3/16" squares each of four colors:
  A: dark eggplant
  B: dark red
  C: light eggplant
  D: light red

Pair up the dark squares (A and B) and the light squares (C and D) together so you'll have 5 sets of each pair.

Draw a diagonal line on one side of each pair from corner to corner with a chalk or Frixion pen. Chain stitch a ¼" line on either side of drawn line. Cut threads between and then along the drawn line of all 10 pair.

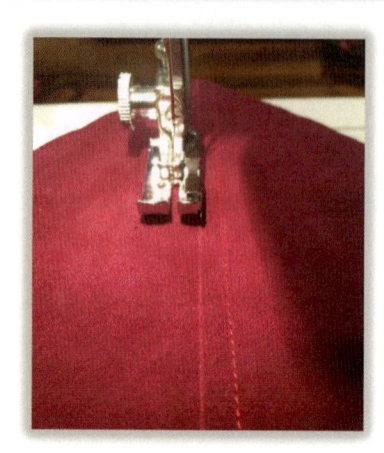

You'll now have 20 half square triangles. Open each and press seams to the darker sides.

Lay them out and line them up diagonally on your mat so that the seam line runs horizontally and cut each square in half from bottom to top so that when you open up each unit, you'll have 40 two-color triangles. 20 light and 20 dark units. I cut them two at a time.

Play with the different ways you can lay them out and find which you like best. I put the darks on the left and lights on the right as shown below.

To attach the units, first fold the white square in quarters (not diagonally) and finger press so that you have lines to match the corners of each triangle to.

Chain piece going around the square: Start with the upper right triangle and with RS facing and the point of the triangle lined up with the finger pressed seam line, stitch with a scant ¼". Repeat for the remaining 9 blocks. Finger press to the dark fabrics. Then attach all the lower right triangles for all ten blocks. Finger press, etc.

Chain piecing around the square makes the process faster and you won't get confused and sew the wrong triangle to the wrong side. In theory.

Trim and square up each unit to 8.5". Sew five squares together twice to make 2 panels for either side of the quilt. Make sure that all the dark triangles (or matching units depending on what you decided) fall to one side of each strip. The strips should measure 8.5"x40.5". Align the strips so that the dark (or same side) patches fall to either the inside or the outside of the sides of the quilt. If you look at mine, I decided to have all the darker patches fall to the outside so that it created a nice border on either side. This will be the orientation for the Broderie Perse application.

Step 2: Broderie Perse.

Find a fabric that has floral motifs that are about 4" in size. This will give you room to center the flowers in our little white canvas and quilt around them.

Lay out the fabric WS up and cut a square of Steam a Seam to cover a chosen flower. Remove the paper and place fusible side down. Press for 5-10 seconds. Let cool. Cut the square out of the fabric and then fussy cut the flower with small, sharp scissors. The fusible web will keep the edges from fraying.

Peel off the gridded paper and center the flower in the diamond keeping in mind the orientation of the strip. Press with a hot steamy iron for about 5 seconds.

Repeat for all 9 white center diamonds. You can use all the same flower or different coordinating flowers depending on the fabric you chose. Make your quilt sandwiches and get ready to ditch and quilt.

Step 4: Quilting.

You'll be joining with a sashing so you don't need to worry about leaving the ½" space on a joining side. Start by using your walking foot and a thin white thread such as Aurafil to ditch the diamonds. That's all the ditching you need to do to stabilize the piece. I didn't ditch the seams of the colored triangles as I wanted those to appear as one unit. Baste the long edges 1/8" from the edge. So far each section has both linear and free motion quilting designs so we'll continue that concept throughout the quilt.

Free Motion the Flowers

Attach your free motion or darning foot and set your machine up for free motion quilting. You can work an applique stitch around each shape as shown on page 77 or choose to do a little something different. I "thread painted" the details in and around the flower and then echoed it once with the same color:

With white, repeat the leaf motif you quilted around the flowers in the large diamonds outside the large orange square in Sections 2.

Here I used white Mettler thread for the background and yellow and orange Mettler for the detail stitching in and around each of the flowers.

Linear Quilting

Quilt a linear pattern on the colored triangles leading to the flowers. I did mark the lines here as I was stitching at different angles and wanted to relax and quilt without thinking. In the diamonds between the white floral motifs, I used a ruler and a Frixion pen to mark ¼" lines. At the end of each mark, I continued the line at an angle that runs parallel to the white diamond. Note that these lines are spaced further apart due to the angles at play here.

Attach your walking foot and quilt the drawn lines, piggybacking on the ditched seams and the seam allowance for each section. Each large triangle can be stitched with one thread.

I used bright red Mettler for the light section and dark eggplant Mettler for the dark.

Step 5: Trimming and Attaching.

Since we'll be joining with a sashing, we can trim these panels flush with the batting and backing. They measure 8.5" wide by approximately 40." Leave a bit extra on the short ends for now. The main piece that we'll be attaching these to measures 39." This actually works out perfectly, because I wanted an additional border attached to the quilt on the sides of Sections 3 (unmarked sides) so that the MP we have so far sits in a frame. I could have done this while working Sections 3, but with the uncertainty of how much shrinkage would occur with the quilting, I left it off just in case. To build up the MP so the 40" panel fits, cut four backing strips 1"x39" and four strips of fusible fleece .5"x39." Fuse the fleece strips to one half of all four strips:

Line up the pieces so that the RS of the strips are placed on either side of the top of Sections 3 of the MP with the fusible on the bottoms so you won't sew through the fusible. Match up all raw edges and stitch with a ¼" seam. Press strips up and away from the quilt and baste the tops closed with a 1/8" seam allowance. Repeat on other side.

This side is now 40" to match the 40" panels.

Set aside the Section 4 panels while we add the sashing to the marked sides of the MP. Take the two 1.5" strips and fold in half lengthwise WS together. Line up the RS of the 1" strip with the MP and the raw edges of the folded strip on top of that as shown:

Match up all raw edges and stitch with a ¼" seam allowance. Turn over and press up only the back strip, leaving the folded front strip faced down for now.

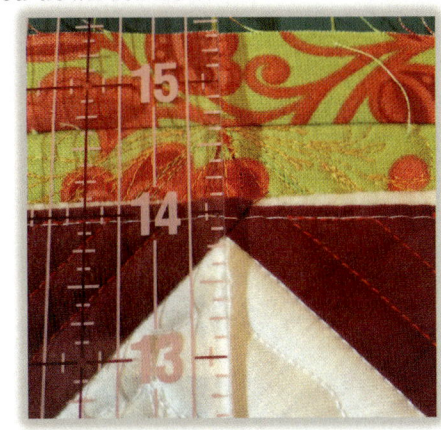

Looking at the photo above, you can see that before attaching the panel, we have to line up the points of the middle diamond of Section 4 to the large point of the square on the MP. Hold the Section just below the top of the back sashing strip so you can line it all up with a ruler. Then slide it up and pin in place. This is the reason we didn't trim the short ends to the exact measurement yet.

With a walking foot, attach the panel with the Section 4 facing up so you don't cut off the tip of the diamond. Trim the short ends flush with the MP. With front facing up, press the folded flap up towards the new section. Pin and hand stitch in place with applique stitch.

SECTION 5:
FLOWER BASKETS, X-BLOCKS AND APPLIQUE.

Since adding Section 4 to the sides of the quilt, we have established its orientation, especially if your flowers have a right side up appearance like mine. The center of the MP is very light, the sides are still on the light side with the white centers, so to get a slight visual effect of courthouse steps, we'll be using darker fabrics for the top and bottom Section 5.

> **Materials.**
> **Fabrics:** Milan print; scraps of the Cherrywood fat quarters, black and a bit of white.
> **Backing and Batting:** two 14"x 60" of both (you'll have to cut three 14" strips and piece the backing.)
> **Freezer paper and supplied templates:** starch, freezer paper, mini iron and Hera marker for turning.
> **Threads:** Aurafil for piecing, Mettler for quilting

Step 1: Center Blocks. Make Two.

Since the applique shapes are going to be stacked on top of each other, we'll be using the freezer paper heat-turned method as we did for Sections 2 to eliminate bulk.

Cut two 12.5" square backgrounds out of the dark print fabric. Fold in quarters (not diagonal) to mark the center. Set aside. Get out your heat turning set:

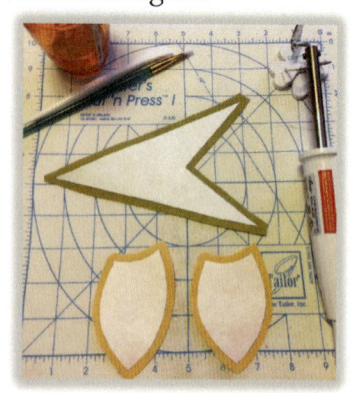

Starch or Best Press, Hera marker, acrylic paint brush, mini iron and pressing surface.

Step 2: Freezer Paper Applique

You'll be using the templates on the next page and following the instructions for heat turned applique on pages 96-99.

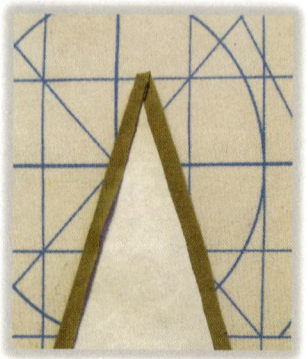

Begin by brushing the first seam allowance with starch and press it down with the iron.

At these sharp points, finger press the opposite side of the point before applying starch to that side. It gives the correct folding angle so you don't get off track. Then continue pressing down the rest of the seam allowances overlapping the fabric folded at each point with accordian pleating.

For each block, you'll need four of the arrow shapes and five yellow petals (use the two given for all 5). No need to turn under the short edges of the petals; they'll slide right under the circles. Trace each shape on the shiny side of the freezer paper with a Sharpie and cut out on the line. Each template can be used about four to six times. Some will stack a few pieces of freezer paper and then cut the shape so the template is thicker. I find that the heat of the mini iron doesn't penetrate all the way through multiple layers on the second or third use, so I just use one and deal with the slight shrinkage in the paper that may occur. Make a 2.75" and a 1.5" circle for the centers and fifteen 1" circles for berries. Use perfect circles templates or mylar or cardboard templates and follow the directions on pages 23-24.

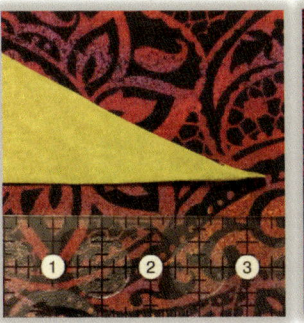

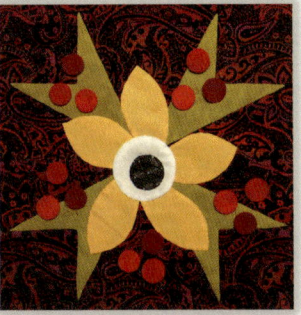

Place the arrows. Center the points together at the cross of the folds. On the outer corners, place a ruler so that each side is 3.5" from both outer edges as shown. Place the petals on the arrows, then the center circles. We'll be echoing the shapes and then stippling the background this time so glue down the pieces (except the 15 red berries) and then hand applique in place. You don't have to worry about stitching the parts of the shapes that are under any others. After the block is quilted, stitch the berries on.

Step 3: Basket of Flowers
Make 4 Blocks

Although this block looks complicated, it is very easy. Not a y-seam to be found. Choose colors from your fat quarter scraps. You'll need 4 colors of red, 3 colors of green and a bit of white and yellow. For the vase, I used brown and for the sides, I used what was left of my Milan print (I already cut for the whirlpool block given below). I used black for the dark triangle at the base of the vase.

Cutting instructions for four blocks:
A: Brown: Cut four 3 1/4" squares;
   cut once diagonally (8 patches).
B: Print: Cut eight patches 2 7/8"x7 3/4"
C: Black: Cut four 5 5/8" squares;
   cut once diagonally (8 patches).
D: Brown: Cut four 8 1/8" squares;
   cut once diagonally (8 patches).
E: Burgundy: Cut six 3 1/4" squares;
   cut once diagonally (12 patches).
F: Dark green: Cut eight 3 1/4" squares
G: Dark red: Cut eight 3 1/4" squares
H: Medium green: Cut six 3 1/4" squares
I: Medium red: Cut six 3 1/4" squares
J: Light green: Cut four 3 1/4" squares
K: Light red: Cut four 3 1/4" squares
L: Yellow: Cut two 3 1/4" squares
M: White: Cut two 3 1/4" squares

Don't cut F-M diagonally yet. We'll make half square triangles. It goes a bit faster.

Pair up Squares F&G; H&I; J&K; and L&M:

Place a ruler on each paired square on the diagonal and draw a line from one corner to the opposite corner. Chain piece these by stitching a seam 1/4" on either side of the line.

Cut the squares apart, cut on the drawn lines and press seams to the darker fabric. Follow the key below and sew the half square triangles in strips as shown:

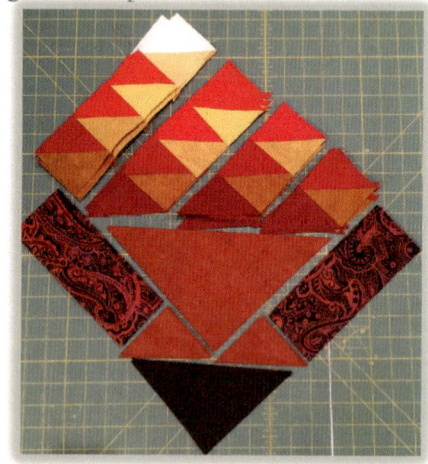

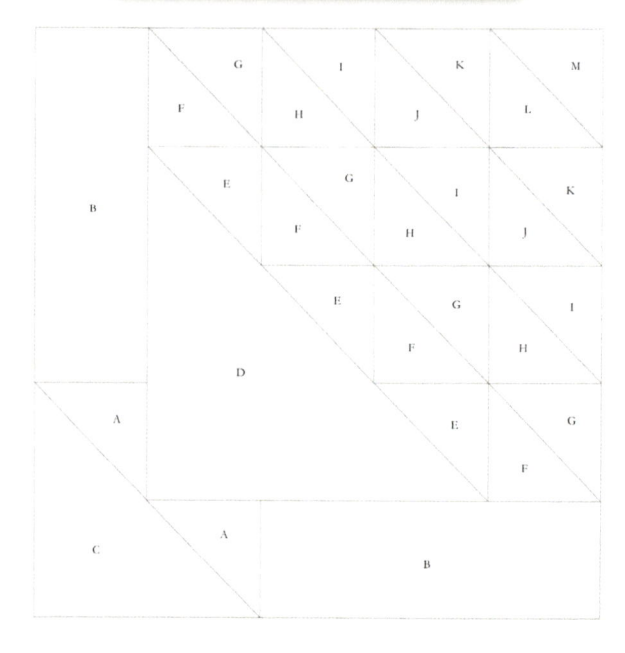

108

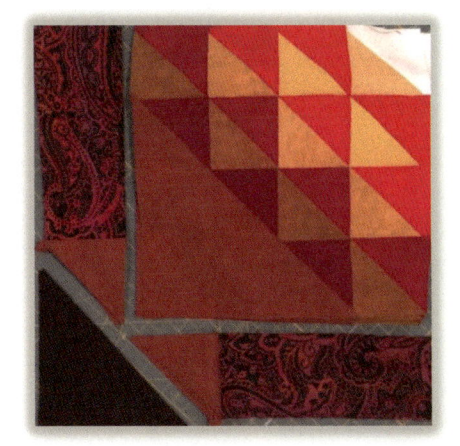

Then stitch the rows together and add the large brown base of the vase. Clip all dog ears and loose threads as you go.

Sew the A patches to the short ends of the background fabrics (patch B) and then stitch the B combo strips to either side of the vase of flowers. The last step is to stitch the black triangle corner to the vase.

Trim the four squares to 12.5" blocks. Set aside.

Step 4: Whirlpool Blocks
Design Decisions

This one gave me some trouble. It's an easy enough block to construct, but the color variations within the block are vast and with the bold colors I'm using, the placement dramatically changes the look of the whole quilt. I pieced the blocks to look like the colors shown on the left, thinking that the orange square would mimic the large center square. Makes sense, right? Then I decided I didn't like it once it was placed in the quilt. My eye goes straight to those bold orange boxes. So I ripped it out and tried many different ways before I finally decided on the Xs. Thankfully, I kept an editing eye on it before it was quilted and added to the MP.

It is my hope that by sharing these bits of my journey to building quilts this way, you will see another person's design process. It is not meant to confuse or scare you into believing that there is only one way to make it. Trust your instinct and make it to please YOUR eye. You may find that the orange squares are perfectly fine and use them. Remember, this is your project. Make it for yourself.

It is essential to look at your quilt from far away. A design wall is helpful in viewing your quilt as a whole. I have a wall in my studio that I hot-glued enough 12" corkboards (Amazon.com) to fill almost the entire wall. If you don't have space for that, lay it out on the floor or outside on a tarp and snap a picture like I did here. Then you can study it for a while before committing.

Close up the squares looked great. From a distance, those bright orange squares make the quilt feel squeezed in somehow. I tried them in the corners, which gave great visual balance, but then the basket of flowers blocks looked odd. No way am I ripping those out. And plus I really like them in the corners. However, I am willing to rip out the whirlpool blocks to make myself happier. It's all part of the process.

Cutting directions are below, but before that, here are a few different block configurations made just by rotating the half square triangles within. After making the half square triangles with the instructions given, you can play with them and decide on what you like the first time:

They are all so pretty, and it would be fun to make one quilt with one block, made in different ways. That's how the design process works and how a series of quilts can be born. One idea leads to another. Again with the open journal. But even looking at the blocks, it's hard to decide which one fits best in the quilt. So you have to play with positioning them in the quilt spot. It's a bit time consuming and at times annoying (especially to your friends and family from whom you will be asking for opinions over and over again), but if you pretend like you're constructing a puzzle or playing a game, it becomes more fun. Like anything else, it's all in the way you look at it.

If you have EQ7, you can kind of play with layouts and color, but until you have the exact colors and fabrics being used, it's not easy to get the exact look of the whole quilt. But with those programs, you can get a basic idea

After an hour, I decided on the X Blocks.

Also, keep in mind that when these get quilted and added into the quilt, it all looks better. Right now it's stark and weird because there are no stitches to break up the colors. You'll get the hang of it.

Make four 10.5" blocks and add a 1.25" strip of dark print to the tops and bottoms to be able to sew them to the 12.5" blocks on either side. A 12.5" width would make the section too long.

Cut 3 3/8" squares out of these colors to make four blocks:
Orange and Dark Print: 16 squares each. Pair up.
Dark and light purple: 8 squares each. Pair up.
Yellow and Black: 8 squares each. Pair up.

Follow the directions for making half square triangles on page 108. Once all your squares are cut apart and pressed, you can play with the orientation. When you've picked a favorite, sew the squares in three vertical strips and then sew strips together to make the blocks. Stitch all the blocks from this section together to make 2 identical sections.

Step 4: Quilting.

Stitch the blocks together in your chosen order. Before sandwiching these two long sections, make sure you mark the side you're joining and trim so that you have straight edges on that side. There are three distinct blocks going on within these sections, so that calls for different quilting motifs. Make your sandwiches. Smooth out the back, then the batting, then the tops. Place about 6 pins on each long side. To make sure it's all smooth on these long pieces, I'll hang them vertically with pins in the top and pat down to make sure there isn't any excess fabric between the pins. You may have to repin in a couple of places. Place blue tape covering the ½" of the joining side to be safe. We are not using sashing.

Start by ditching the seams that join the blocks. Remember to start and knot ½" from the joining side and end beyond the outer edge. Smooth with your hands and then baste the non-joining side 1/8" from the edge. Don't worry about basting the short sides. Remove the pins. Ditch around the end baskets (don't stitch in that ½" space) and the colorful patches that make up the X blocks. I did all this in black Aurafil (and black bobbin) as my dark print has a black background.

Quilting the Center Flower

With black threads and your free motion foot, echo quilt once around the outer edges of the applique flowers and arrows about ¼" away. Then work a simple relaxing stipple in the background. As long as I was stippling, I decided to continue the same stipple pattern in the background of all the blocks. It's a great pattern to quilt on a busy background and brings continuity to the entire section. With black still attached, work a spiral shape in the center of the flower.

I did no marking on this block. With yellow, work lines that travel up and around each petal with one thread, piggybacking the white circle between them. With green threads work simple long integrated leaf shapes, each with its own thread. With purple threads, work long and short stems with small swirls at the ends around the black center. Don't choose red for this. It looks eyeballish enough! Hand applique stitch the red berries.

NOTE: I quilted both Section 5 at the same time. As soon as I was done ditching one, I went on to the next. When I stippled the first panel, I stippled the next. After the center flower on one, I did the second one…etc. This way, what you did the first time will be repeated easier as it's still in your mind. It took me about 11 hours to quilt both sections. But the quilt grows much faster with two pieces!

Quilting the X Blocks

You may have a different configuration for this whirlpool block and that's okay. As always, quilt it with any inspiration you may have or you can follow what I did. The X is very graphic and begs for linear quilting to offset the stipple done in the background. With a walking foot, I worked ½" lines running toward the square in the middle and on the middle orange diamond, did ½" cross hatching that brings the eye to the cross hatching done in Sections 3.

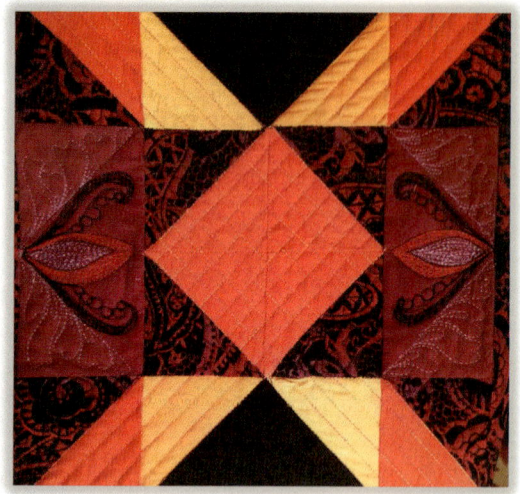

For the purple rectangles, I copied the motif from the center section and worked some bloopy feather shapes outside of the scrolls. The only free hand marking I did beforehand was the flame shape and scrolls. Remember, that if you draw a line that you don't like, you can simply brush it away with chalk or iron it away if you used a Frixion pen.

Quilting the Flower Baskets

Since I used brown for the basket, I thought it would be fun to work a wood grain pattern. Practice drawing it on paper without lifting your pen. It's a fun and easy line to quilt so once you've drawn it out, no marking is necessary. Note the two green dots at the point. I started in the center and worked left and then with a new thread went right.

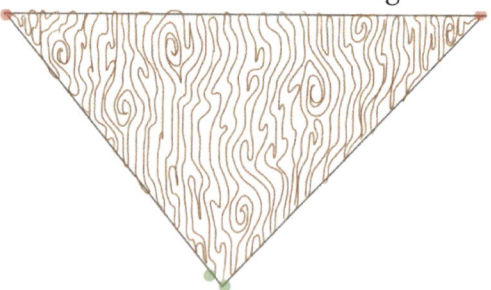

You can change the density of the wood grain, or any quilting for that matter, depending on how you want it to look but also on how much or little you want your piece to shrink to fit the MP. That's a little trick to put in the back of your head while quilting. I went pretty dense with my wood grain to get a bit more shrinkage, but play with your drawing to find your perfect grain.

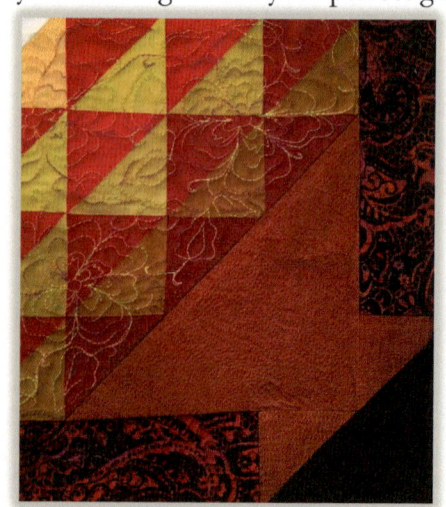

For the colorful floral portion of the block, copy the corner motif we did in white for Section 2 but in a multi-color thread. Above the wood grain line, quilt some little green grassy stems that reach up and fill the space between basket and flowers. The black triangle was stippled with the background stipples.

Step 5: Trimming and Joining.

Press the panels so they're as straight and flat as you can make them. On these longer, larger pieces, I like to trim the joining side first, making sure I have a straight line to sew. That way, when trimming the other side, you can straighten up the section based on the sewing line. It is easier to keep the entire quilt straighter once these are joined. Remember to leave that ¼" extra batting and backing on the joining side when trimming:

Once the joining side is trimmed, flip it over and square up the outer edge. The panel should measure 12.25." Next, trim the excess of the short sides. Don't trim it up exactly to the size of the MP edge until it is stitched on.

Fold back the batting and backing, line up the center of the flower applique block with the "V" of the larger center square (top layer only). Pin like crazy. This quilt is heavy. Things tend to slide apart. Stitch:

NOTE: I'm not gonna lie. It's challenging to keep the joining sewing lines straight when pieces get this heavy. If you don't sew on a large table (like me), think about getting dog grooming arms (Amazon.com) to attach to your table (picture on 120) to keep the weight off the machine. These help tremendously. I also use them when I free motion quilt larger pieces, which is rare anymore since I really love quilting in smaller sections. However, times do call for whole cloth quilting, so I break three of these out and place them around my tiny table.

Once the joining seam is sewn, open it up and press the seam from the back. Now look at the front. Are there places where the seam got a little wobbly and is under the ¼" seam allowance? It's ok to take it back over to the machine and stitch over that section to make the line straighter. I do it all the time.

Pin the backing out of the way and trim the batting so it butts up against the MP batting. Go slow and try not to cut the backing fabric. If that happens, take a piece of interfacing and iron it to the WS so it doesn't fray. Give it some "stitches" on the RS later. Yes, I've done that too. Frowny face.

Once the batting is trimmed, fold under the excess backing fabric so that the fold extends just beyond the joining seam. Press down, and hand applique in place while binge watching Downton Abbey or some other fabulous form of entertainment.

SECTION 6:
FREE MOTION BORDERS

The quilt has a lot going on with both graphic and floral shapes and contrasting colors. For Sections 6 and 7 we'll be framing the center with classic black and the sashing color to pull it all together. Rather than adding additional motifs and shapes, we will simply be stitching around and between the motifs of the printed fabric. Once you get into the zone, this is incredibly relaxing while being a great way to practice getting more accurate and comfortable with free motion quilting.

Materials.

Fabrics: Two border strips 5.25"x65"; Two black strips 1.5"x65"
Backing and Batting: Two strips 8"x68" each.
Threads: Aurafil for piecing and quilting

Step 1: Piece, Sandwich and Quilt

Stitch the long edges of the floral and black strips together and that's all the piecing we need to do for this section. The detail for these panels is all in the quilting. Make your quilt sandwich and pin along the long edges. Ditch the seam, stitch a line on the black strip ¼" away from the seam line, smooth out the floral strip and baste the long edge.

Attach your free motion foot and with the background color of the border fabric, outline the motifs of the fabric and work stipples to travel between them.

You can do this with one thread. Take it slow and do your best. Don't worry about hitting the outer lines of the motif lines exactly. When using the background color, it all blends in and the eye will look at the piece as texture rather than the individual line. If you were to use the motif color, missing the line would be much more obvious.

Quilting the lines of and around the motifs of a piece of fabric is one of the best ways to practice free motion quilting. There are no seams to bump into and the shapes are already established for you. Relax and get into the zone. Soon you'll see there is a zen like flow to this. It's easy to get sucked in. After every 15 or 20 minutes of quilting, get up and stretch.

Once both panels are done, trim the black joining edge with that extra ¼" of bat and backing and join them to the MP as instructed on page 113.

SECTION 7:
FREE MOTION BORDERS WITH APPLIQUE

For the final sections, we'll be closing up the floral border and adding a black quilted background that will hold the applique at the top and bottom of the quilt. This is fun as there is lots of room for play. Looking at the center of the quilt, we have free reign to finish it off by duplicating some of the motifs we've already done.

Materials.

Fabrics: Foral print: two strips 5.25"x69"; four strips 1.5"x5.5"
Black: two strips 1.5"x59"; two strips 10.5"x69"
Backing and Batting: Two strips 17.5"x71" each.
Threads: Aurafil for quilting floral; Black Mettler for grid quilting on black border
Blue Painters Tape: one inch for quilting grid lines

Step 1: Piece and Sandwich.

Sew a floral 1.5"x5.5" strip to each end of the black 1.5"x59" pieces. The strips should measure 69." Stitch the long edges of the 5.25"x69" floral pieces to those strips and then stitch the 10.5"x69" to the other long edge of the floral strip. The whole piece measures 16.25"x69."

Make the quilt sandwich. You'll need to piece the backing by cutting four 17.5" strips from backing fabric and sewing two short ends together. Measure out to 71" and trim the excess. To cut batting for these large pieces, lay it out on the floor and place the backing at an outer edge. Smooth out and cut out with scissors. This is much easier than trying to manage cutting batting with a rotary cutter.

Flatten and smooth the sandwiches with your iron. Pin every 12" along the long sides. Hang them vertically on the design wall and use gravity to further smooth out the wrinkles. Repin where needed.

Ditch the two seams and stitch a black line ¼" from the floral edge on the little black joining strip. Smooth out the fabric and baste along the non-joining edge and the short sides.

Step 2: Quilting.

If you lay this newly assembled section next to the MP, you'll see that the black strip of Section 7 extends about ¼" on each side of its coordinating border of the previous section and that the whole piece extends ½" on either side. This was my best guess on the size that allow for shrinkage based on my plan for the quilting. It will be very close. If it's slightly off, we can always add that strategically-placed applique piece or stitching to make it all fit. It's ok. The pros do it all the time.

As you can already imagine, you'll be doing the exact same quilting on the floral borders to give the whole frame some continuity. Be careful here though. Remember that ½" space you need to leave on the joining side. You may want to reach for the blue tape and cover that portion. It's really easy to find yourself in that quilting zen and get carried away. You can quilt just over the seam line on those little 5.5" floral tabs and get close to the tape.

For the black background for the applique, keep it simple. I've referenced the classic Coco Chanel quilted bag pattern here. And who doesn't love a bit of Chanel in their quilts? I'm tempted to put those white double Cs right smack dab in the middle. Poof! Instant designer quilt. But I'm not a copier so I'll just enjoy the subtle hint of one of my favorite designers.

One inch blue painter's tape is the best material for quilters to make a classic diagonal quilted grid. You can use the bars that come with your walking foot when quilting lines in the same direction, but when using the same thread and zigzagging back and forth as you'll be doing here, the bar ends up on the wrong side every other line. You can remove that hassle by just placing two pieces of tape down side by side at a 45 degree angle and leapfrogging them every time you stitch a line. You can reuse each tape about 8 times before you'll need to tear off a new piece due to fuzz. And speaking of fuzz, the batting lint attached itself so quickly to the black, it was driving me crazy. I trimmed all the excess batting off the 3 non-joining sides while I was quilting it. The little batting lint I got from the fourth side actually came off with each tape removal. Another bonus of using tape. From time to time, check your tape line to make sure it is still at a 45 degree angle by placing a 45 degree triangle in the space or checking it with your 6"x24" ruler lines. You should be able to quilt each directional line pattern in one thread. Travel in the 1/8" seam allowance or in the ditched seam to get to the next line. To eliminate some of the excess turning, keep in mind you can use your reverse button to travel between lines or to get yourself in the correct needle position so you can stitch right between the tape guides in certain cases.

Once both panels are finished, you are ready to create some wonderful applique pieces that bring the whole quilt together in one fantastic piece.

Step 3: Applique.

I made the same freezer paper templates and followed the same method for the tulip and vine motifs from pages 97 and 98 of Section 3. I thought it would be the most striking way to fill the black top and bottom borders. I also stitched on a few orange squares and made white, purple and red circles to coordinate with the berries from the previous sections.

Rather than pre-planning the entire layout and marking where each shape would go, I like to cut and make all the shapes I think I need to fill an area and then play around with the pieces designing as I work. When I find a partial layout I like, I'll pin the pieces in place and continue working until I am satisfied that the area is well covered, leaving enough negative space so all the pieces really stand out.

Step 4: Trim and Join.

Since I cut the excess batting and backing around the three non-joining sides, we just have to trim the joining side with that extra ¼" of batting and backing extending from the top layer. The final trimming of the other sides we can do when we square up the entire quilt before the binding.

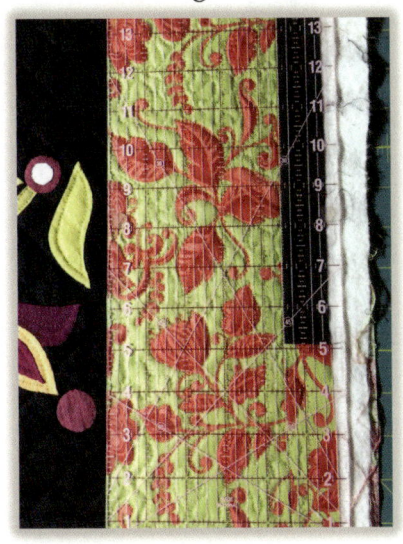

Place RS together and fold back the backing and batting of the Section 7. Match up the 1" black border ends with the vertical borders from Section 6 located 5" in from the outer edges of each side. Pin and/or clip in place. Stitch the top layer of Section 7 to the MP and trim excess batting, fold the backing over and stitch in place. My black border lines came out nearly perfect. I hope you have the same good luck!

FINISHING:
TRADITIONAL BINDING

Lots of people I know cannot stand this part, but I just love it. No more thinking. You can rest your mind as the hard work is done. Plus there is nothing like that last stitch that completes the quilt. Talk about a sense of accomplishment. And what a great reward!

The quilt measures approx. 66"x93." To get the binding length, add 66+66+93+93+ extra 18" for bias joining and corners. Divide that by WOF (42") and you get approximately 8. Cut eight 2.25" strips out of your binding fabric (I used the backing). Piece with bias angles to reduce bulk:

Place short ends of two strips as shown, draw a line from corner to corner and place a pin. Make sure when you open up the strip, it will be a long continuous line. If you draw the line in the wrong direction, it won't work.

Stitch all the lines and cut the corners off with a ¼" seam allowance. Press the enormously long binding strip lengthwise with WS together:

Did someone order the spaghetti?

Begin at the bottom of the quilt and line up the raw edges of the binding strip to the raw edge of the quilt. Don't bother pinning. You can hold it with your hands as you stitch. Start 6" away from the end of the bias strip.

Work your way to the first corner and stop ¼" away from the edge. Turn the quilt slightly and work a few stitches to the corner and off the quilt. Raise the needle and pull the quilt away so you can work the miter.

Lift the binding up so that a right angle is formed and the raw binding edges form a continuous line with the next quilt side.

Fold the strip back down so the top of the fold lines up with the quilt top. See pin:

Turn and continue sewing from top edge.

Continue making your way around the quilt and follow the mitering instructions for all four corners. When you approach the beginning of the strip, stop 10" from end. Overlap the end of the binding strip on top of the beginning and trim it 2 ¼" (width of binding strip) from the point of overlapping:

Pull the quilt slightly away from and to the left of the needle so you can fold and manipulate the quilt to join the ends on the bias. This is important if you don't want a bulky bump on the edge of the quilt.

See how the quilt is accordion folded a bit making it easier to place the ends together on the angle as you did when you originally joined the strip pieces? Pin ends together as you did when joining the strips and stitch it on the diagonal as shown:

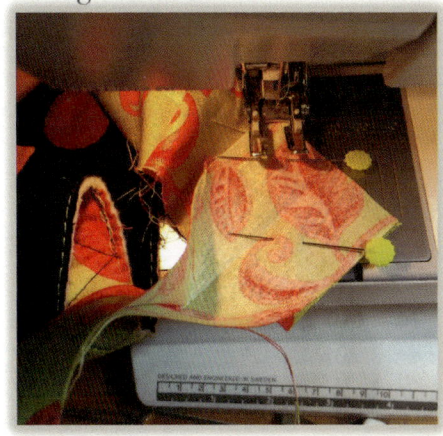

Refold the bias strip and it will snap into place and lie flat along the edge of your quilt. It's like magic. Rejoin thread where you stopped and continue sewing, overlapping the start point. Press the edges up and away from the quilt with your iron, put in 3 good movies and hand stitch down on the back.

Hooray! You have just completed another large size quilt on your domestic sewing machine! This project is pretty straightforward without a lot of hand embellishment so I know I'm already happy with the end result and it will need nothing extra but a label and a sleeve for photographing.

Labels

People now and in the future will want to know who the maker of the quilt is and where it came from. The most pertinent information to include is your name and address. Other helpful information is the size, who it was made for and/or why, materials used and techniques employed. Some artists include their inspiration. My method of making a label is to type up all the information that I want to include on Word and then print it out on an 8.5"x11" piece of fabric that has been fused to an 8.5"x11" piece of freezer paper. This runs through an inkjet printer nicely. I like the idea of including a photo of the quilt, original photo or inspiration and including that on the label.

Sleeves

If you want to hang your quilt on the wall or enter it into a show, you'll need to construct a 4" sleeve for the back. Cut a strip of backing fabric 8.5"x1" less than the width of your quilt (you'll need to piece it). Turn the short edges under ¼" twice, press and stitch in place. Fold it lengthwise WS together and press making a crease in center. Open up and refold the edges in to meet the center crease. Press each side so those two fold lines get good creases. Unfold and refold RS together lengthwise and stitch the long sides together. Turn tube right side out. Orient the tube so the stitch line is in the direct center and lies against the back of the quilt. The two creased lines become the top and bottom lines that you will pin in place and hand stitch to the quilt usually an inch or so below the top. The tube is not supposed to lie flat. The ½" ease of excess fabric is so the sleeve will be able to fit over a hanging rod or slats. You can also make a bottom sleeve so it hangs straight.

CONCLUSION

My favorite thing in the whole world is to learn or invent different textile art techniques and share them with other people. The way I see it is "what good is knowing how to do all this stuff if you can't pass it along?" It is a privilege to be with someone who reaches that aha moment when they learn something new. That's why I love teaching.

I have enjoyed creating these two projects for the purposes of sharing my unconventional approach to quilt making. If you have worked mostly traditionally, it might be difficult to wrap your mind around working with improvisation. But try it - not all of your quilts have to be worked this way. It's just another method amongst the many.

I get asked about my process for some of the things I've made, and often the answer is that I don't exactly remember as I'm not consistent in the way I go about creating. I sort of problem solve my way through a design with the skillsets I have. I'm a huge proponent of taking classes and learning techniques no matter how long you've been quilting. The bigger your toolbox is (literally and figuratively), the more confidence you'll have in executing a vision that is begging to be realized.

I am in love with the tiny house movement that is happening now. The idea of surrounding myself with only the belongings that I use and cherish, instead of filling a huge house with lots of stuff, appeals to me like never before. I'm currently exiting out of lots-of-stuff mode and it feels amazing to get rid of and let go of what we aren't using. It is freeing us up to travel lightly and live life in each moment without being tied down to material things left behind. I guess that's why I find comfort and love in hand stitching and working on the go and in small spaces (see my work space above). A longarm machine just won't fit in our future tiny home so I had to come up with an alternative style of quilting. Keep watch for Quilt As *Inspired*, Volume II. I've got some fun new "games" to share.

I so hope that you have found inspiration and a few new tools for your own quilter's toolbox to go forward in creating your own designs. Trust your instincts, have fun, and always be yourself.

Until next time, I'm yours in hugs and stitches,
Ann

16693985R00070

Printed in Great Britain
by Amazon